Integrated English Language Development

Supporting English Learners Across the Curriculum

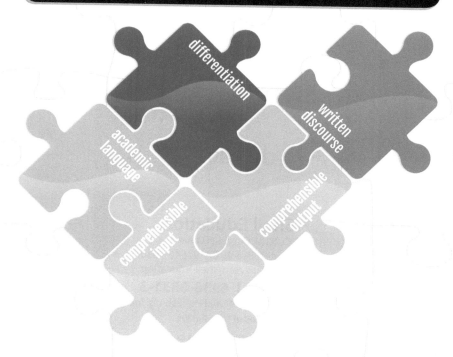

Author
Eugenia Mora-Flores, Ed.D.

Foreword by
Jessica Villalobos, M.A.Ed.

SHELL EDUCATION

Publishing Credits

Corinne Burton, M.A.Ed., *Publisher*; Conni Medina, M.A.Ed., *Editor in Chief*;
Aubrie Nielsen, M.S.Ed., *Content Director*; Véronique Bos, *Creative Director*;
Robin Erickson, *Art Director*; Andrew Greene, M.A.Ed., *Editor*;
Kevin Panter, *Senior Graphic Designer*; Dani Neiley, *Assistant Editor*

Image Credits

All images are from Shutterstock.

Shell Education

5301 Oceanus Drive
Huntington Beach, CA 92649-1030
www.tcmpub.com/shell-education
ISBN 978-1-4938-8831-3
© 2019 Shell Educational Publishing, Inc.
Printed in USA BRP001

Table of Contents

Table of Contents *(cont.)*

Acknowledgments

When I have the honor of writing a book, I am often asked, How do you do it? How do you find time in your busy schedule to write a book? My answer is always the same—I am blessed to have family and friends in my life who help make it all happen! This book and the others I have written could not have been possible without the help and support of my family and the amazing teachers who welcome me into their classrooms.

My husband, Rudy, and children, Emilia, Aidan, Samantha, and Adan have always been patient with me when I had to write and brought me joy to get through the writing blocks and tired typing hands. My nieces, Isabella and Juliana Mora, thank you for spending your vacation time helping me with graphs and charts; your technical expertise was invaluable. Love you girls!

Angelica Machado, you have always opened the doors to your classroom and taken risks with your instruction. Thank you for always trying out all of the strategies and sharing the excitement of your students as they engage with one another and learn through new practices. This book and all of the others would have never been possible without you. Thank you, thank you, thank you!

To the teachers I have had the pleasure of working with for over twenty years, from Moreno Valley, San Antonio, Montebello, San Diego, Los Angeles, and the many other districts I have been a part of, your enthusiasm for learning and growing in your practice keeps me motivated and makes me want to do more for students. Thank you for being part of my journey and for your ongoing support in my work in integrated ELD.

As the daughter of immigrant parents, I am honored to be able to work with the teachers and families of students from diverse backgrounds and experiences. Your struggles, your successes, and your never-ending dedication to your children gives me hope that all students will receive a high-quality education, one of high expectations, rigor, and authentic care.

This book was possible because my parents believed in me and did everything they could to provide me with an education that was provided by teachers who not only cared, but expected the best of me and others like me.

—Eugenia Mora-Flores

Foreword

I grew up in a Spanish-speaking household, with the belief that education was an equal opportunity for all. If you worked hard enough, you could be anything you wanted to be. Never did it cross my mind that barriers existed within the educational system itself that would prevent me from reaching my potential as an English learner. It wasn't until I became a teacher that these systemic inequities began to make themselves clear.

After spending 15 years in secondary bilingual classrooms, I became senior director for the Department of Language and Cultural Equity at Albuquerque Public Schools. It was through my work that I had the opportunity to cross paths with Dr. Eugenia Mora-Flores, and I knew immediately that she was the right person to help our district further our work of removing obstacles for English learners. She came to us at a critical time when we were beginning a paradigm shift in our work with ELs—defining the lens through which we view these students and reinforcing the added value they bring to the classroom.

In this inspiring text, *Integrated English Language Development: Supporting English Learners Across the Curriculum*, Dr. Mora-Flores connects theory and practice, clearly outlining the role language plays in the classroom. This book will take you beyond differentiation in the classroom, delving deeper into how we can guide English learners to think metacognitively, use the language of critical thinking, and understand the resources they already possess. Throughout this text, Dr. Mora-Flores emphasizes the importance of building bridges for students between what they already know and the experiences they engage in within the classroom.

Now that I am a district leader, it is my vision and obligation to help correct the inequities that persist with English learners. The premise of Dr. Mora-Flores's book embodies the message that is at the core of the paradigm shift underway at Albuquerque Public Schools: *Language access leads to equity in education*. In order to change the learning outcomes of this historically underserved student population, our work must be transformative.

The Language and Cultural Equity team at Albuquerque Public Schools has developed a set of core beliefs around English learners. I hope they further inspire you to absorb the contents of Dr. Mora-Flores's book, as these core beliefs reflect the urgency of our work and our commitment to equitable educational outcomes for students.

- **In order to create equal outcomes for English learners, our work must be transformative**. Because our students will become the problem-solvers of tomorrow, we believe students should read and learn in order to broaden perspectives, deconstruct meaning, analyze and form arguments, and critically think.

- **Educators' beliefs are not abstract concepts; they shape policies and practices and have clear consequences in our everyday teaching and learning**. We need teachers who are "warm demanders" raising the bar and believing their students can do difficult and challenging work.

- **English learners, and all students, need rigorous curriculum that is student centered**. With the right supports, English learners can engage in rigorous learning experiences where students are doing the "heavy lifting" and the teacher is guiding and facilitating.

Meeting the needs of our English learners is serious business, and we must recognize that the very lives of our students depend on our willingness to create opportunities for equal access to language and content.

To everyone reading this book, you are in for a wonderful journey through the work of Dr. Eugenia Mora-Flores, a leading expert in her field and a wonderful human being. Her book will equip you with best practices in ELD, give you a better understanding of how to support ELs across the curriculum, and, most importantly, it will give you the tools to transform your practice.

—Jessica Villalobos, M.A.Ed.
Senior Director of Language and Cultural Equity
Albuquerque Public Schools

Une force est nécesaire pour faire du travail. Toutes les fois qu'on utilise une force pour déplacer quelque chose, on travaille. Selon l'action et la force nécesaire, le travail peut être facile ou difficile. Au fil des ans, les gens ont inventé des machines pour les aider à faire le travail.

All content-area teaching and learning is replete with language. If we can see the language demands of our discipline, we have taken the first step toward guiding students to learn our content and develop language. If you skipped over the passage above, take a moment now to read it. Were you able to read the text? How were you able to read it? What prior knowledge did you draw upon? Some of us might have relied on our foundational literacy skills such as decoding the text using knowledge of phonics (letters and sounds) or our knowledge of grammar and punctuation. When we are exposed to any content, be it through written text or oral forms of communication, we are immediately presented with language.

Students must access language in all content areas. From the moment they are presented with information, they are processing language. But accessing the language is just the beginning. Look back at the opening passage and ask yourself, what is the text about? What information is it trying to convey? Is it an informative piece? Is it trying to convince or persuade me of something? What argument is the author making? What is the main idea or purpose of the text? All these questions are drawn from our desire to learn the information. When we are presented with information, we start by accessing the text, and then we dive immediately into trying to make sense of it. We have to interpret what the text says; therefore, we have to interpret language—how the author uses words to convey meaning, what words mean in the given context, and how language is used to argue a point of view or perspective.

Every content area requires students to understand language, and in the current educational culture, students need to understand it at a level of critical analysis and evaluation. And the learning doesn't end there. As teachers, when we engage students with content, we expect them to be able to share with us what they have learned. This *output* of their learning can come in many forms, from written to oral communication. If I asked you to write an abstract summary of the passage above and be prepared to engage in a critical discussion in which you present and defend your point of view with information from the text, that would require a great deal of language. The goal would be for you to learn the information presented, but language learning would also happen along the way.

The role language plays in learning in all content areas gives this book its purpose. My goal for us as teachers of English learners is to become explicitly aware of the language demands our content areas require of our students and for us to be able to support the access, interpretation, use, and production of language across the curriculum. The goal is not to ask teachers of social studies, science, math, art, physical education, and all other disciplinary areas to become English teachers, but to help content-area teachers implement the strategies necessary to teach their subject matter in a way that all students can learn. And if language is involved in how the content is taught, then language needs to be supported as well. My hope is that this book will demonstrate how language can become a seamless, natural part of teaching any content.

The opening discussion introduces us to the technical understanding of language across the curriculum, but we cannot lose sight of the social-emotional implications of this work as well. Think about your own experience and feelings as you tried to read and interpret the opening passage. How did you feel? Were you able to successfully access and interpret the language and then use it to produce written French to demonstrate your understanding of the passage? Your interaction with the French passage was a low-stakes experience; your ability to successfully understand the passage did not have significant implications for your future as a student or teacher. Yet our English learners are held to the expectation that they not only learn the content, but also be able to successfully demonstrate their learning in English. English learners are challenged with the task of trying to problem-solve their way through content while simultaneously learning a new language. It is not a choice, but a requirement for our students to learn the content. They are held accountable for their learning through formative and summative assessments, including those developed by teachers, districts, and state and federal departments of education. There are implications for lifelong success and future educational opportunities. I shared that my goal is to help teachers see language in their teaching, but I also strive to help teachers *want* to see and support language across the curriculum. Language is there, and we as teachers must be ready to guide language while students are learning content.

Chapter 1 begins by examining our students' language needs and drawing a distinction between designated and integrated English language development (ELD). To begin understanding what it means to support English learners across the curriculum, we continue with a discussion about how to define academic language in **Chapter 2**. We look more closely at what it means to differentiate for English learners in **Chapter 3**. I present a framework for thinking about differentiation through the exploration of comprehensive learning objectives. **Chapter 4** continues with a discussion about how we can help students access content to make learning comprehensible. This discussion includes accessing oral and written forms of language to support English learners in developing both content knowledge and academic language. The attention given to making content accessible is followed by an equally important focus on integrated ELD with a discussion about comprehensible output in **Chapter 5**. The interactions between input and output when learning language are critical for students to have successful language learning experiences. When students are asked to make meaning of what they are learning, they are further required to demonstrate their learning. **Chapter 6** goes on to discuss the challenges of written discourse. I share suggestions for deconstructing language to support students in reconstructing written language across the curriculum. I conclude the book by reflecting on our practices and dedication to supporting all students in the classroom. I am inspired by teachers who continue their learning and continue to work tirelessly to meet the unique needs of all learners in our classrooms, particularly in supporting English learners to reach high levels of academic success.

All strategies I share throughout this book are approaches that I have personally used as a teacher, coach, or consultant directly with English learners at various levels of English language development. There are many strategies available to support English learners in integrated ELD. I have selected those that have not only been successful but some of my students' and teachers' favorites. You may find new ways of adapting these strategies by making them your own, or you may find yourself using them for other purposes to achieve success with your students. Everything I share has helped me guide English learners to feel successful accessing, processing, and producing the English language. It is my hope that you will be able to implement these strategies so that you can foster the same academic and linguistic confidence in your classroom.

Part I:
Foundations

What Is Integrated ELD?

Anticipation Guide

Decide whether you agree or disagree with the statements below.

- Learning a new language and new content is a complex process.

- English learners need language support throughout the day and across all curricular areas.

- It is the responsibility of the English language development teacher to teach English learners English.

Getting to Know Our Students

To guide learners is to know them. It is important for all students to feel connected to the classroom and believe their teachers understand what they are going through and truly care about their learning. Angela Valenzuela (1999) led a three-year study that explored the academic experiences of Latino students in Texas. One of her core findings was the need for teachers to exemplify and demonstrate *authentic care* if students were to succeed academically. According to Valenzuela, authentic care "views sustained reciprocal relationships between teachers and students as the basis for all learning" (61). Students need to believe their teachers care about them and their success in school.

To get to know my students, I like to begin the school year with an activity called *I Wish My Teacher Knew....* To complete the activity, provide each student with a large sticky note. In the middle of a large sheet of chart paper, write the sentence starter *I wish my teacher knew....* Have each student complete the sentence on his or her sticky note. I always encourage my students to be honest and share anything they want. Usually, students share personal learning preferences, interests, and needs. I provide them with the option of putting their names on the sticky notes. Figure 1.1 shows a third-grade example of a heterogeneous class of English learners, gifted students, and students with special needs. The samples show how students said, "I wish my teacher knew karate," and "I wish my teacher knew how to cook." These sentences give the teacher insight into students' interests. Another student shared, "I wish my teacher knew what I'm going through." Another shared, "I wish my teacher knew I am smart." These are clear expressions of students' desires for their teacher's empathy. Students need to feel valued for who they are and encouraged to express themselves freely.

Figure 1.1 | I Wish My Teacher Knew...

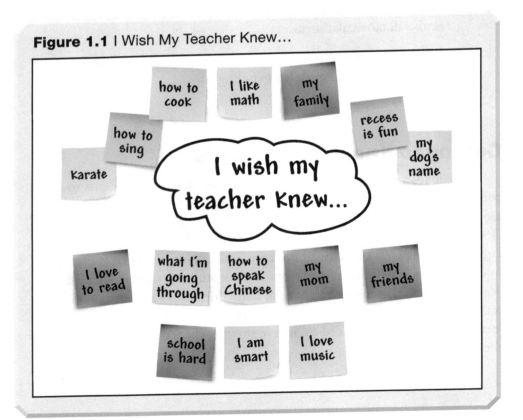

I have seen many teachers use this activity as a formative assessment after teaching a mini-unit of study. For example, after a unit on fractions, one teacher led her students in completing an *I Wish My Teacher Knew* chart to understand students' perceptions of what knowledge they had gained or areas of continued struggle around the topic of fractions. Students were not required to put their names on their sticky notes, so this activity gave the teacher a collective understanding of her students' comfort level with fractions. Used throughout the school year, this activity can help students feel that their teachers truly care about them and their learning.

A more traditional practice for learning about students is through surveys. A variety of surveys, including interest surveys, reading and writing surveys, and learning preference surveys, can be used in the classroom or sent home to continue to get to know students. For younger students, asking them to complete an interest survey in class can be difficult. Some may not yet have the language and literacy skills required to read and understand the questions and provide clear written explanations. In these cases, meet with students one-on-one in an interview format and have them share their answers orally. The survey can also be sent home so families can help students. Figure 1.2 is an example of a home interest survey that was used at the beginning of the school year in a kindergarten class. Older students can complete the survey in class or at home for homework. Figure 1.3 (page 18) is an example of a reading interest survey that was used at the beginning of the school year in a fourth-grade class.

Figure 1.2 Home Interest Survey

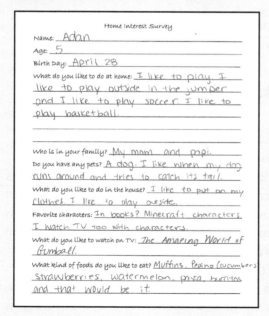

Figure 1.3 Reading Interest Survey

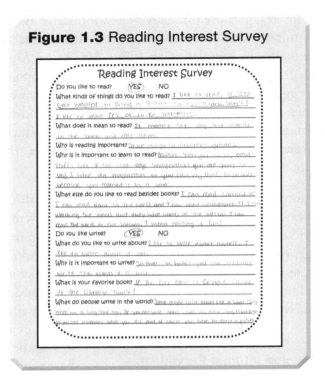

Connecting what we know about students personally to what they are learning in school makes the learning experience meaningful for students. Ultimately, these connections can lead to higher student outcomes.

Learning from Students: Connecting Theory to Practice

I had the opportunity to work with some of the most knowledgeable and passionate educators I have known in the areas of English language development and supporting English learners. Drs. Lilia Sarmiento, Dolores Beltran, Cristina Cortez, Sylvia Lezama, and I were part of a team of educators who spent years exploring how students navigate language in school and how teachers support the language learning experiences of English learners. In my work with these amazing educators, we learned from students and listened to their stories and experiences in the classroom as English learners. What fascinated me about this work was that the very theories and research we read about were all voiced in their own words and experiences. As part of a study, we conducted a survey with students, asking them a range of questions about their experiences as English learners in high school classrooms. For their answers, they were able to draw from their years in school as they worked hard to learn language and achieve academic success. The following responses clearly demonstrate that students can teach us a great deal about how to support them as English language learners. The quotes below show students' experiences in their own words, juxtaposed with corresponding second language acquisition theories and big ideas teachers can take away from their messages.

"Teachers should speak with them [ELs]. Give us time to talk. To share ideas and we can talk in English. We should have time to talk to our partners and share whatever we are doing in class and talk about what we did."

Comprehensible Output (Swain 1985)

Merrill Swain argues that language is developed when we attempt to express language in oral or written forms, and we receive formal and informal feedback from others through normal interactions, causing us to "fix up" our language until we are understood. This feedback process helps us learn to express ourselves in a comprehensible manner. Therefore, we need to provide students multiple and varied opportunities to use language through meaningful interactions with others.

Deep Processing Theory (Long and Porter 1985)

"Teachers should make us read more in English. They should make us talk with our partners. That way, we can learn to talk more English."

Learning is a complex process. To develop language, it takes multiple exposures to the language and ample opportunities to interact with the language. To hear a word or phrase used orally or in written form can create an initial familiarity, but multiple and varied written and oral interactions with it will increase the likelihood that language will be retained and ultimately used. Deep processing theory reminds us that to develop academic language, we need to see, hear, read, and write language often and for a variety of purposes.

Interactionist Theory (Craik and Lockhart 1972)

Interactionist Theory is grounded in the belief that to develop language, we need to interact with other people who are more knowledgeable (or in this case, more linguistically adept) than the language learner. The theory focuses on the relationship between a child's environment and their exposure to language.

Affective Filter Hypothesis (Krashen and Terrell 1983)

When learning a new language, Krashen and Terrell argue that students should feel comfortable taking risks with language, knowing that they are immersed in an environment that supports language learning. A classroom that establishes a culture of acceptance and values diversity can give students the confidence to be themselves and understand that language learning comes with many trials and errors. Krashen and Terrell believe that an environment that creates a lot of anxiety and stress in language learners can raise the "affective filter," which does not allow language to "get in." It keeps students from being open to learning and can become a barrier to learning. A low "affective filter" is felt when students know that they will be supported in their language learning process, and they are open to expressing their ideas and interacting with others. These opportunities help students to acquire language.

"That you are not supposed to get mad when they are barely learning English."

"That he or her don't need to be pressured because if you pressure them they are going to lose control and not study."

Common Underlying Proficiencies (Cummins 1981, 2000)

Based in the Interdependence Hypothesis, Cummins explains that although languages can appear and sound very different on the surface, students learning new languages bring with them common underlying proficiencies, or skills and conceptual knowledge, that transfer across languages (Cummins 1981, 2000). For example, if students already know how to summarize a text in their native languages, they don't need to learn how to summarize again. They already possess that skill. However, they would need to learn the surface language, or how to express the skill, in the new language.

"Some teachers are good teachers, they make connections with the Spanish—for example, conección sounds like connection."

Input Comprehension Hypothesis (Krashen and Terrell 1983)

Input Comprehension Hypothesis examines the idea that humans acquire language in only one way—by understanding messages or by receiving comprehensible input (Krashen 1985). The i + 1 formula symbolizes how comprehensible input works: messages in the language must make sense, ideally, just beyond the competence of the learner, who must strain a bit cognitively to understand.

"Maybe the students could be a teacher."

Cultural and Linguistic Responsiveness (Hollie 2012)

This theory describes the confirmation and support of the home culture and language to guide students to success in school and society.

"I think that [teachers] need to know their [students'] culture, their language and find a way for [students] to learn quicker."

Academic Language Development (Nagy and Townsend 2012)

Academic language can be defined as the discipline-specific and generalizable conceptual language that is used in school. It includes but is not limited to the knowledge of the vocabulary, syntax, semantics, and pragmatics of language used across disciplines to demonstrate learning in academic contexts (Nagy and Townsend 2012).

"Teachers should make school about learning English and also learning Spanish and also they should make P.E. English and Computer Lab English."

Cognitive/Academic Language Proficiency (CALP) (Cummins 1981)

This refers to comprehensive understanding of language meaning in an academic setting. It includes listening, speaking, reading, and writing about subject area content material.

I am reminded of my own language learning experiences and how those experiences have been my foundation in supporting my own students. As a child, I can remember a variety of experiences that helped me learn English. My parents are both immigrants from Mexico, and for my brothers and sisters and me, Spanish was our first language; it was the language of our home, our family. My first memory of language learning was in Spanish. My *Tía* Lucy has a high level of academic Spanish. She and her sister (my *Tía* Feli) were two of only three women to graduate with a degree in Engineering from a prestigious university in Mexico. Unfortunately, as female engineers and as immigrants in the United States, they were unable to use their degrees at the time, so they worked in the fields and factories. Their Cognitive/Academic Language Proficiency (CALP) in Spanish was at such a high level that I remember always being corrected by my *Tía* Lucy. If I didn't use the proper formal tense of a verb when speaking to an adult, she would correct me and make me say it again correctly. When I wrote my first syllabus in Spanish at the University of Southern California, she was my editor. She taught me to stop translating text from English to Spanish, and to begin by thinking about it in the language I was going to use. This experience was frustrating as a child, but rewarding as a language learner.

As one of six children in my family, Christmas presents quickly turned from individual gifts to family gifts. We were given a lot of board games. At the time, I didn't realize the real gift that we were given. Looking back, many of the games were vocabulary games (Password, 10,000 Pyramid, Scrabble®, Blurt!®, Whatzit?™, TriBond). We learned a lot about words and word meanings by playing English board games as a family. Later, as a teacher, I realized how important these games were to my development and learning of vocabulary. These experiences and many more had a significant impact on how I came to develop language, both in my first language, Spanish, and my second language, English.

I remind teachers that we all were, and continue to be, language learners. From my own experiences learning a second language, there are strategies, practices, tips, and tricks that my teachers shared with me or that I discovered myself that we can use in our work as teachers of language learners. This book is an attempt, as a teacher of English language learners, to share with other teachers my journey in language. After twenty-five years in the field of education, I have come to value what I have learned from my own teachers, my students, and the thousands of teachers I have had the privilege of working with.

Designated and Integrated English Language Development

Knowing about language helps teachers understand the role of language across the curriculum. Daily, teachers work to ensure that their students access, understand, process, and produce language to be successful in school. For centuries, the focus has been on how to teach students English in isolation through programs such as English as a Second Language (ESL) and English Language Development (ELD), with the hope that as students continue to develop English, they will be able to keep up with content taught, in English, across the curriculum. A strong focus on a dedicated ELD instructional time led to the development of ESL and ELD curricula and supplemental materials to specifically guide language instruction. Designated time for teaching language is provided through a range of structures and approaches, including pull-out ESL programs and class time allocated for English learners to receive language intensive English instruction. During these times, English language is at the forefront of the instruction. The core objective is language, guided by English language development standards.

The article "English Language Development: Guidelines for Instruction" by Saunders, Goldenberg, and Marcelletti (2013) presents key elements found in successful, research-based designated English language development programs. Though this is an area that warrants further study, they explain the importance of designated ELD and successful practices. An ELD program's primary goal is to develop English language skills that foster communicative competence and communication abilities. They suggest that this type of designated ELD instruction should continue until ELs have attained advanced levels of English language development, which can take an average of four to six years. How language is taught in designated ELD and which resources and materials are used to teach language has evolved. Lessons in ELD are to be taught through rich content connected to topics and concepts students are learning in other content areas. It is about language *in use*, not simply *knowledge about* language (Saunders, Goldenberg, and Marcelletti 2013). Language remains the primary objective, but instead of teaching language in isolation, teachers pull language from text, videos, and other media to meet the language objective. For example, if a teacher is going to teach students about the purpose and proper usage of adjectives, he or she can pull examples from texts related to topics being studied in other content areas to teach the language skill. Teachers can even source the materials being used in the content areas for this very purpose.

The difference between how the text is used in designated ELD versus content-area instructional time has to do with the focus of the lesson. If a teacher were to use a book about the heart and lungs during science, the focus would be on the content and knowledge related to the parts of the body and the functions of the heart and lungs. Using the same text during ELD instruction, the teacher would use the text to identify how the heart and lungs are being described using adjectives and pull out examples of sentences to deconstruct and reconstruct. Students can then go on to learn more adjectives for describing the heart and lungs and practice using adjectives in writing. The focus during designated ELD is to make sure students know and understand what adjectives are and how to use them properly. Learning about the heart and lungs is secondary and will not be the focus of the teacher's assessment during this time. But the rich context for learning about language helps students see language *in use* so they can learn *about* language.

Other considerations for designated English language development include instructional time, classroom dynamics, and language proficiency levels. Researchers have found that the most effective designated ELD programs group students by proficiency levels and provide separate, dedicated blocks of time for ELD instruction at students' targeted language proficiency levels. Grouping students together helps teachers focus on the specific language needs of the group. However, these groups should be flexible as the rate of language development varies greatly from student to student. Saunders, Goldenberg, and Marcelletti (2013) further argue that English learners should not be segregated by language proficiency levels or English language learner classifications for the entire school day; they should be mixed with a range of students at different English language development levels, including English-dominant students. Other instructional considerations are provided in the following table.

Designated English Language Development
• Instructors provide deductive and inductive approaches to explicit instruction.
• Teachers emphasize academic language as well as conversational language.
• Teachers give a greater focus to academic language, especially at the middle and upper levels of proficiency (to minimize plateau effect).
• Instructors incorporate reading and writing, but listening and speaking should be emphasized.
• Teachers integrate meaning and communication into instruction.
• ELD is in English, with primary language support limited and used strategically.
• Teachers should provide corrective feedback, both in recasting and prompting.

Though these efforts have led to ELs developing English, what educators have come to learn is that language instruction alone is not sufficient for ELs to successfully engage in all content areas throughout the day. Traditional ESL/ELD programs focused heavily on oral language development and did not prepare students for the academic language demands across disciplines. Content instruction is academic language instruction, and it provides opportunities for Academic Language Development (ALD). Language is how knowledge and content are shared. Language is how we interpret information and transfer information to share our thinking. To do so across disciplines requires a range of specific language demands, including common functions, forms, and vocabulary. ESL and ELD instruction is necessary as it sets a foundation for language to be further developed across the curriculum, but ESL/ELD alone cannot provide English learners with the language support they need to be successful in school.

Integrated English Language Development (I-ELD)

Integrated English language development is understanding the language demands of our content instruction and providing intentional language support to help students access, interpret, and produce language. Making the language demands of our lessons explicit (comprehensible) and guiding students to use language to share what they have learned is at the core of what all students must do to be successful in school. Integrated ELD is content-area instruction; it simply calls out the need to be more intentional about language instruction to ensure successful content-area lessons.

The need to focus on supporting English language learners throughout the day, across curricular areas, is not new to classrooms across the country. Teachers have worked hard through a range of supports from Specially Designed Academic Instruction in English (SDAIE) strategies to ELD/ALD strategies that promote oral language development. For over 25 years, I have seen teachers use SDAIE to help make their content instruction comprehensible for students, and the work started many years before I entered the field of education. Dating back almost 40 years, theories and researchers in the field of second-language acquisition brought to light the understanding that in order for language to be developed, it must be understood. If students do not understand what they are learning, the opportunity to both develop language and learn the content can be negatively impacted. Stephen Krashen and Tracy Terrell (1983) presented a hypothesis called the Input Hypothesis, also referred to as Comprehensible (Input) Hypothesis, which captured this notion. If language is not understood by the learner, it cannot be learned. The message must be comprehensible if language learning is to occur. This work led to a range of strategies and practices that teachers employed to support their English learners to make the content they were teaching understood by students.

Popular approaches included SDAIE strategies that helped intermediate language learners access language and content by making the content comprehensible. SDAIE also included opportunities to use language to further support language development. It was the intersection of strategies for comprehensible input and output. Initially, the main focus was on input, but strategies have developed over time to include comparable output strategies. Other comprehensive planning models, such as Sheltered Instruction Observation Protocol (SIOP), were developed to support teachers with SDAIE strategies and comprehensible input practices throughout a lesson. The lesson design includes key elements such as content and language objectives, generating prior knowledge, opportunities for interaction, wait time, academic language support through sentence frames, or other language cues. Tools such as the SIOP planning model began as an observation tool to measure teachers' implementation of sheltered language instruction and then evolved into a lesson plan model to guide teachers in their work with ELs (Echeverria and Short 2010). The focus on input was helpful, but soon teachers saw in their classrooms that helping students understand the content was not enough. If students are to fully develop their academic English, teachers need to provide comprehensive support.

Merrill Swain (1985) argues for comprehensible output, which involves the need to provide opportunities for students to interact and engage in exchanges of language (oral and written) to maximize language development. People provide feedback to others through interaction until their messages are understood. Though Swain's work dates back to when Krashen and Terrell were discussing comprehensible input, it was not until recently that Swain's work has been valued because of the increased demand for students to be able to demonstrate academic language through a range of oral and written academic experiences. Students have to be able to communicate their ideas. With the rise of rigor in thinking in classrooms, students are expected to interact with one another and engage in academic conversations that require high levels of academic language. Classrooms have begun to see the need for more student discussions. In the past, English language development strategies included rich input and output through popular strategies such as Project GLAD®, which includes "professional development in the area of academic language acquisition and literacy…that specifically target and promote language skills, academic achievement, and cross-cultural skills" (Project GLAD® 1990, n.p.). But where Krashen and Terrell focused on input and Swain focused on output, there was another school of thought that asked, is it really the relationship between the two? Based on the work of Lev Vygotsky (1978), Interactionist theory supports the idea that students learn language when they interact with their environment and develop language from interactions with fluent, more proficient users of language. Interactionist theory brings input and output together. Supporting students as they interact with content, language, and one another could provide a richer language and learning experience. By providing a comprehensive approach to content-area instruction for English learners, teachers can find a place for all the previous work they have done to support ELs by bringing their work together in integrated ways. Dutro and Moran (2003) noted that SDAIE was not enough for supporting English learners and focused on a need to guide the academic language involved in learning. "Current research strongly suggests that a more comprehensive model is needed. The literature makes clear that explicit instruction in English and how it works—vocabulary, word usage, grammatical features, and syntactical structures—must be included" (Dutro 2015, n.p.). Through a range of practices, such as the use of visuals, realia, and graphic organizers, teachers have been making great efforts to help English learners understand the content at hand.

What has changed recently is the growing focus and understanding that language is integral to the academic success of all students and must be made explicit. Standards have shifted across the country toward integrated approaches that include seeing how language *and* literacy are a part of all teaching and learning. Revisions to standards are helping teachers understand the role that language plays in students' learning across the content areas. English language development standards in states such as California have been written with directives to implement them through integrated approaches.

Integrated versus Designated English Language Development

We do not teach language for the purpose of language alone; we teach language to help students access, gain, and communicate about knowledge across all content areas. Language is seen as part of all teaching. Though these integrated approaches are part of designated language instruction, they are equally a part of how language is integrated in all content-area instruction. What differs in integrated language approaches from language-focused instruction is that content remains the core objective of the teaching and learning experience. From the beginning to the end of a lesson, the main purpose is the content objective at hand. Language is used to successfully meet the content-specific objective, and language is learned as a by-product of the language-rich, authentic learning experience. But content remains the focus of an integrated ELD content-area lesson. All content-area lessons are integrated language lessons because all subject areas require language to achieve the learning objective.

SDAIE, ELD, and ALD all work together in *integrated* approaches to language development for English learners. During content-area instruction, students are provided a range of supports that guide their ability to make sense of what they are learning. These supports help students to process and interpret content and express their learning in diverse ways. Throughout the day, students are encountering and learning academic language while also being expected to use it, which makes integrated English language development (I-ELD) an essential part of a student's academic success. Content-area teachers all work toward helping English learners access their content that is presented through language, and they also help English learners demonstrate their learning using academic language. Therefore, integrated ELD becomes the responsibility of all teachers. Not all content-area teachers need to be language teachers, but they should be aware of the language demands of their content and support students to access and use it successfully. Designated English language development (D-ELD) is a protected, designated time of day when English learners are provided "critical English language skills, knowledge, and abilities needed for content learning in English" (CA ELA-ELD Framework 2014, 115). During designated ELD, it is recommended that students are grouped by their English language proficiency levels to provide targeted language support. Teachers work from their English language development standards that outline the specific needs of English learners at different levels of ELD. Where English learners are provided targeted support during designated ELD, it is recommended that throughout the rest of the instructional day, English learners interact with and be placed in classrooms with a range of English learners and English-dominant classmates. The table below summarizes the core differences and similarities between D-ELD and I-ELD.

Differences Between Designated and Integrated ELD

Designated ELD	Integrated ELD
Students have common English language development levels. They are grouped by proficiency level.	There are mixed English language development levels (Saunders, Goldenberg, and Marcelletti 2013).
English language development standards are the goal; content-area standards are used to guide content and context for language instruction.	Content-area standards are the goal; ELD standards are used to guide language support.
Language is taught through rich content.	Language is scaffolded and supported in content instruction.
Reading, writing, listening, and speaking are included with an emphasis on speaking and listening.	It includes reading, writing, listening and speaking equally.
English is the medium of instruction.	English is the medium of instruction, but primary language can be used as a scaffold to access content.
It occurs at a designated time of day.	It is taught throughout the day as part of all content-area instruction.

Integrated English language development provides English learners with comprehensive support throughout the day. They receive specific language instruction and have language support as part of all content-area lessons. Figure 1.4 offers a visual representation of I-ELD. This book will provide educators and educational leaders with a clear understanding of how language is part of content-area instruction and what teachers can do to support English learners while remaining focused on the content objectives.

Figure 1.4 Integrated ELD

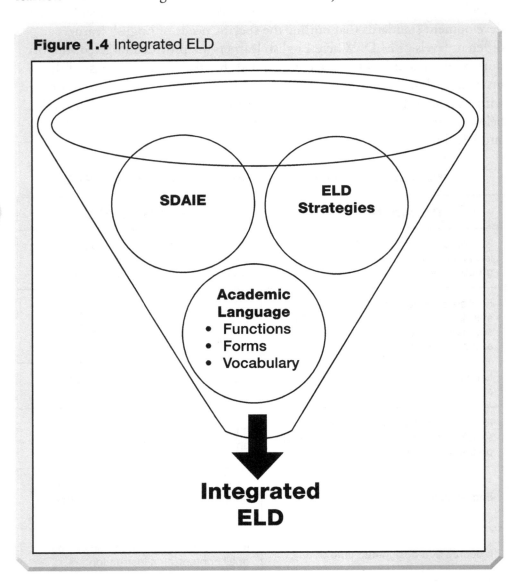

Moment of Reflection

1. What was learning language like for you? What helped you learn language and what did you struggle with? How can those experiences shape how you support English learners?

2. How has language been made explicit for your students across curricular areas? Is there room to work as cross-content area teams to ensure that English learners are being supported throughout the day?

3. What does designated and integrated ELD instruction look like at your school and in your classroom? What areas need improvement? How can you work as a school to provide a comprehensive language program for ELs?

Chapter 2

Academic Language

Anticipation Guide

Decide whether you agree or disagree with the statements below.

- Students need to learn sophisticated language structures and vocabulary to be successful in school.

- Academic language is the vocabulary of my discipline.

- It is the English teacher's job to teach English learners academic language.

Why Is Academic Language Important?

We often tell teachers that supporting English learners in developing academic language is their responsibility because language is part of their teaching and student learning. What we do not always understand is what it means to support academic language development across the curriculum. To support academic language, we must first be able to define it. What is academic language? How can we define it explicitly in the lessons we teach across the curriculum?

Academic language is the language we use in school to access content, interpret content, and produce content to express what has been learned. Content in these contexts can be presented through a range of media forms. The range of sources and resources that are used to present content involves a complex set of language patterns, vocabulary, syntax, and discourse. As we learned in our opening experience in this book, language is present in all learning experiences. We never stop learning language. As teachers, we are exposed to new words for understanding old concepts and new words for new ideas developed in the field, and we continue to strengthen the fluency with which we use known language. This is the reality of students' experiences in school and beyond. The access students have to knowledge outside the classroom today has shown the expansion of academic language beyond the classroom. Later in this chapter, the academic language registers and experiences students engage in outside of the classroom will be discussed.

Saunders, Goldenberg, and Marcelletti (2013) define academic language as the specialized vocabulary, grammar, discourse/textual skills, and functional skills associated with academic instruction and mastery of academic materials and tasks. This definition recognizes the importance of being able to master academic materials and tasks. Academic language is a tool to access the academic material and successfully complete all tasks related to demonstrating learning. Academic language is necessary for students to be successful in school. Students must use language that is authoritatively presented, informationally dense, and highly structured (Schleppegrell 2004).

In our classrooms, it is important to be able to define the academic language demands of our lessons explicitly for students. We cannot simply say to students, "Make sure you use the formal language structures for expressing your learning in our class." We need to make that language concrete. Throughout the chapter, we will explore the four elements of academic language: function, forms, vocabulary, and fluency.

Content, Thinking Skills, Resources, and Products

Every lesson should always have an objective that identifies what students are expected to learn and be able to do. Objectives can be developed by defining four core parts of a learning experience: content, thinking skills, resources, and products. All parts of an objective are important to make sure students understand what they are expected to learn. Equally important is *how* they will learn the content and demonstrate that they have met the objective. The standards define the content. Standards state exactly what students need to learn. Some standards are written as performance standards and can provide further information on how students are expected to demonstrate the content. The content cannot exist alone because it needs a thinking skill to accompany it. Likewise, teachers don't just teach content; teachers ask students to do something with that content. For example, we might be required to teach about ancient civilizations in history-social science, but what is it that we want students to do with that content? Should students be asked to identify, describe, compare and contrast, evaluate significance, or find evidence to prove something? A thinking skill can help us guide students through the content in a variety of ways. The resources provide us with access to the content. How will they learn it? What will be the source of the information: a video, textbook chapter, article, lecture, or peer discussion? The end products then show what students have learned, and they encourage students to demonstrate how they have met their objective. The end products can vary and should connect directly to the content and thinking skill. Figure 2.1 (page 36) shows a range of content, thinking skills, resources, and products based on the following math standard: *Compose two-dimensional shapes (rectangles, squares, trapezoids, triangles, half-circles, and quarter-circles) or three-dimensional shapes (cubes, right rectangular prisms, right circular cones, and right circular cylinders) to create a composite shape, and compose new shapes from the composite shape.*

Figure 2.1 Content, Thinking Skills, Resources, and Products

Content	Thinking Skills	Resources	Products
shapes	compose	math textbooks	create paper shapes
rectangles	identify	trade books:	drawings—dry erase, sand sketches, paper sketches
squares	describe	*Eye Spy Shapes in Art* by Lucy Micklethwait	
trapezoids	compare		
triangles	distinguish	*Cubes, Cones, Cylinders, & Spheres* by Tana Hoban	cut and paste shapes by category—organizers
half-circles	create		
quarter-circles		manipulatives	compare and contrast organizer
three-dimensional shapes		pictures of shapes	
cubes		three-dimensional shapes	math journal entries—visual glossaries
right rectangular prisms			
right circular cones			
right circular cylinders			
composite shapes			

Using the table, we can see the variety of options for guiding students to meet the standard. Some students may need to take a step back and identify the shapes and draw examples, while others may be ready to compare and contrast shapes and complete a graphic organizer. Using the table, teachers can create a range of learning objectives that meet the needs of their students. The table also shows the vocabulary, both content and academic, associated with the standard. Seeing a learning experience through these four parts of an objective helps us better understand the academic language demands of a lesson.

Language Functions and Forms

The function of language is the purpose for using language. Are we using language to make comparisons, justify our thoughts, state a preference, or ask questions? The function of language frames determines how language will be expressed in oral or written forms. Teaching English from the perspective of language functions helps us identify the language demands of a specific academic task. This perspective includes recognizing and understanding a range of language functions that support academic language proficiency and help students participate in content instruction (Dutro and Kinsella 2010).

Forms, or what are often called sentence frames or sentence forms, are the syntactic structures used in the English language to articulate thinking processes. If students are asked to compare and contrast, their language function connects to the thinking skill; what they are thinking is what they will need to articulate or demonstrate through language, so the function determines the forms. Figure 2.2 (pages 37–42) provides examples of common language functions and forms.

Figure 2.2 Common Language Functions and Forms

Language Functions	Possible Sentence (Frames)	Cue Words		
Agreeing and Disagreeing	I agree with...but...	agree	right	disagree
	I believe...was right when he/she said...but...	believe	wrong but	wrong
	I disagree with...when he/she said...	think	however	in favor
	I am in favor of...			
	I think...was wrong when he/she said...			
	I agree with...However...			
Expressing Likes and Dislikes	I like...	like	adore	hate
	I want...	enjoy	want	do
	I love the way...	love	dislike	don't
	I enjoy...			
	I don't like...			
	I dislike...			

Figure 2.2 Common Language Functions and Forms *(cont.)*

Language Functions	Possible Sentence (Frames)	Cue Words		
Identifying	It smells like... It looks like... It feels like... It sounds like... It tastes like...	**Sensory Words:** looks tastes feels smells sounds		
Refusing	I will not... I do not want to... He or she did not want to... I wouldn't... I didn't... I am not going to...	not would not am not wouldn't won't do not didn't will not did not shall not cannot		
Sequencing	First...then...lastly... At the beginning...next... finally... In the beginning...in the middle...at the end... First...second...third... last...	**Ordinal Words:** first middle then second end later third finally last(ly) beginning next		
Wishing and Hoping	I wish... If only I... Maybe I can... I hope... If I had...then...	**Cue Words:** hope if...then crave wish want maybe perhaps		
Comparing	...is...but...is not ...has...but...does not ...can...However... ...can...whereas...cannot Though...can...cannot	but can/cannot as opposed to whereas is/is not however different		

Figure 2.2 Common Language Functions and Forms *(cont.)*

Language Functions	Possible Sentence (Frames)	Cue Words		
Classifying	...belongs in this category because... ...is part of this group because... I organized the...by... You can group these together because...	belongs part of group	order organize sort	together
Explaining	...is...because... The reason for...is... He or she was...For example... I would like to clarify that...	is/is not because reason	for example make clear	clarify such as
Warning	Don't...because... Be careful not to... Watch out for... Stay away from... because... I warned you not to...	don't be careful watch out caution	inform advise notify alert	stay away warn
Hypothesizing	I think...because... I believe...because... Maybe...is...because... Perhaps...is the reason why... It's possible that...	think believe perhaps	assume possible imagine	maybe
Planning and Predicting	I think...is going to happen because... Perhaps he or she will... Maybe he or she will... because in the text it said...	think believe perhaps	maybe expect guess	see coming

Figure 2.2 Common Language Functions and Forms *(cont.)*

Language Functions	Possible Sentence (Frames)	Cue Words		
Commanding	Begin by... First you will...then... Start by...then...finally... Before you begin...then... I order you to...	start/begin then/finally order	demand command will	should do not
Reporting	It all began when... The incident/event took place... It is/was about... What happened was... The real story is that... It all started because...	tell state describe story details	happened report testify give an account convey	inform recount event/incident
Expressing	I would just like to say... I find... I was thinking... I just had a thought... I have an idea... I am sure that... I realize now that...	think idea thought find/found	sure/unsure state communicate put across	say realize
Obligating	You have to...because... He was forced to...because... It was necessary because... You must...or else...	must force have to	require make	necessary mandatory

Figure 2.2 Common Language Functions and Forms *(cont.)*

Language Functions	Possible Sentence (Frames)	Cue Words		
Evaluating	I would have to disagree with...because... I agree that...but... I think... I decided that... Based on what happened, I believe...	agree disagree decided	accept however further	furthermore think
Expressing Position	I support the idea/position that...because... I would agree that... I side with...because... I do not believe that... because... In my opinion...	support agree disagree	opinion view side with	position
Expressing Obligation	I must... I feel I have to... I believe it is my responsibility to... I should...because...	must obligated should	responsibility duty commitment	requirement have to
Inferring	I believe the author is trying to say that... Even though it doesn't say so in the text, I think... The more I think about this passage, I realize... After reading this page, I think that... I suppose the author is trying to say that...	infer believe think	thought assume understand	suppose conclude

Figure 2.2 Common Language Functions and Forms *(cont.)*

Language Functions	Possible Sentence (Frames)	Cue Words		
Suggesting	I would recommend… After listening to/reading…I suggest… I would advise you to… I propose…	propose advise	recommend suggest	
Criticizing	I don't think he or she should…because… I dislike the way… He or she should not have… I disapprove of the way in which… I commend him or her for… I admire how…	disapprove dislike approve	praise admire commend	congratulate applaud

Vocabulary

Of course, academic language includes vocabulary. Vocabulary can be organized through content or academic vocabulary (McKeown and Beck 2004; Anderson and Nagy 1992). Based on the original work of Isabel Beck and Margaret McKeown (2004), vocabulary can be understood through a tier system, which is a method to understand words based on their purpose and use. Beck and McKeown identified three tiers. Tier I refers to the prior knowledge or acquired vocabulary that is part of the natural language acquisition process. Teachers do not have to explicitly teach Tier I words because students immersed in language will just "pick up" these words through highly contextualized experiences with the vocabulary. For example, I wouldn't need to put a word such as *chair* on my vocabulary list because students hear the word often enough that it will be learned and understood by exposure, as it is used in their everyday experiences.

Tier II words are considered academic vocabulary. Academic vocabulary includes words that are conceptual, high utility, and have high instructional purpose and function. These words are transferable and widely used across all content areas, and they will be heard and used by students often in academic contexts and through varied experiences outside of school. Tier II words serve a critical role in students' academic language development because they are words that help capture what and how students are learning. Moreover, they are used to express thinking across disciplines. I like to think about Tier II words as the words we expect our students to *retain* beyond the lesson at hand. Take, for example, the word *purpose*. This word transfers across all content areas and has high instructional potential. We can discuss synonyms related to the word *purpose* and how they are used in context. When do we use the words *reason*, *point*, *idea*, or *rationale* versus *purpose*? We can explore morphology with the words *purpose*, *repurpose*, *purposeful*, and *purposefully*, and discuss how roots and affixes change or enhance the meaning of words.

We can talk with students about the transferability of Tier II words as they are used in other disciplines. What is the author's purpose? How would you state the purpose of the experiment? What was an artist's purpose for selecting a specific medium? Tier II words are called out as words that we want students to internalize and make a regular part of their academic vocabulary bank when learning across content areas. These words should be the focus of English language arts and English language development vocabulary lessons.

By explicitly studying academic vocabulary words, students will come away learning and understanding a range of words. Given the example of the word *purpose*, once we finish studying that word, students will have been exposed to its synonyms and multiple meanings in context. So even though it is just one word, they will learn and explore in this case possibly seven new words (*reason, point, idea, rationale, repurpose, purposeful, purposefully*). English language arts and English language development teachers are encouraged to be more selective with their words and choose just a few Tier II words. Anderson and Nagy (1992) discuss the importance of developing *word consciousness*, or a curiosity about words and their meaning. Word consciousness fosters curiosity about words students encounter through both incidental and explicit word study. Nagy (2005) continues to explain the move away from focusing on too many words that are not connected to a context or learned through connections with broader concepts. Teachers do not need extensive vocabulary lists if they teach students to learn about words and become interested in exploring word meanings. Vocabulary researchers have presented a range between five to ten words to focus on for explicit instruction (Beck, McKeown, and Kucan 2002). It is not necessary to teach a large number of words each week. As long as they are academic vocabulary words, teachers will come away having taught many more words in the end. Tier II words are conceptual and transferable, which allow teachers to make connections to other words and concepts. Teachers can talk about synonyms, antonyms, and subtle nuances of words as they are used in a variety of contexts. This way, students can go deep in their learning of vocabulary. Focusing on the quality of instruction versus quantity is important in explicit vocabulary instruction.

Tier III is the third classification of vocabulary words. Tier III words are discipline-specific words that are not seen or heard often outside a specific content area. These words have an important role in the content areas because teachers expect students to learn and comprehend them to access and understand the information being taught. Discipline-specific vocabularies, or content vocabularies, are made up of the types of terms that for years were defined as academic language. For example, math words such as *isosceles*, *scalene*, *algebra*, and *algorithm* are academic language, but these words by themselves provide a narrow understanding of what academic language means. As explained above, academic language includes language functions, forms, vocabulary (Tiers II and III), and fluency.

Still, discipline-specific vocabulary remains an integral part of all content-area lessons. I like to refer to it as vocabulary for comprehension. These words are essential for students to understand the content. The question that remains, however, is the role of content-area teachers in teaching Tier II vocabulary. How do teachers and students use academic vocabulary alongside content vocabulary during integrated English language development?

Vocabulary Instruction in Integrated ELD

Content-area teachers have the main objective of teaching their content. Some teachers might argue that they don't have time to teach lengthy vocabulary lessons on academic vocabulary words—and they are right. But I would argue that there is a place for content-area teachers to use academic vocabulary as part of their lessons. Academic vocabulary presents opportunities for teachable moments. When you find yourself talking about vocabulary, and the word you are presenting happens to be Tier II, capitalize on that opportunity. For example, if I were teaching a lesson in science on the systems of the body, I might share with students, "Systems of the body—where have you seen the word *systems* before? Have you used that word in another class?" Then, students can make explicit connections to the terms and the concept. This approach helps students make broader conceptual connections across content areas, and it helps students see that academic language transfers across other curricular areas.

Where does that leave Tier III? Tier III is referred to as the low-frequency, discipline-specific vocabulary that content-area teachers would argue is core to their students' learning. Tier III words include the vocabulary words that are specific to the content or unit of study, and they resurface within the same discipline when students extend their study of a topic. For example, the words *mitochondria* and *cytoplasm* are specific to science when students study cells. Those words are not heard too often outside the discipline of science, and therefore they are considered low-frequency because students will not have much exposure to them outside of the science discipline. However, content-area teachers would argue that these words are critical to the content area and students' abilities to master their objectives. Agreed! These words are at the core of what we teach across the curriculum. We cannot lose sight of their importance for students' *comprehension*. Integrated English language development calls out discipline-specific vocabulary by having students explore their meanings and understand their roles in the broader concepts and topics being studied. These will remain the focus for integrated ELD, but we want to be cognizant of academic vocabulary so that we can make the explicit connections and transfers for students. Figure 2.3 overviews the differences between content and academic vocabulary.

Figure 2.3 Differences Between Content and Academic Vocabulary

Tier III—Content (Discipline-Specific) Vocabulary	Tier II—Academic Vocabulary
Low frequency Discipline specific	Generalizable • High utility • Conceptual • High instructional potential
FOCUS: Comprehension	FOCUS: Retention and Application

Vocabulary Strategies

The focus on vocabulary across curricular areas can be enhanced through vocabulary strategies that give students the opportunity to explore words more deeply. We have historically given attention to words at the surface level: *What is it? What does it mean?* Because content can be very new to students, it is no surprise that we focus on the surface-level meaning. What is a dividend, a circuit, an antagonist, or a civilization? All content areas are replete with words that are new to students, and we need to make sure they know what they mean. What we might consider is how we can help students take those initial ideas and definitions and understand them more deeply. Students can think about related words, conceptual and contextual connections, cross-context uses, and analytic representations of the words themselves. When students can connect words to broader conceptual understandings, it makes the learning process easier (Anderson and Nagy 1992; Nagy 2005). The following strategies can support English learners in extending understanding of words.

Read Around the Word

Purpose: Read Around the Word is a strategy that helps students learn how to use words properly in context. The strategy starts with a Tier II academic vocabulary word and provides students an opportunity to think about how words and their synonyms carry subtle nuances that give the words specific meanings in context. It's best to use academic vocabulary words for this strategy because they are conceptual and have synonyms. Students will learn that not all synonyms can just be substituted from one context to another. They can explore why this is the case and understand the proper use of words based on the context.

Process: Begin by exploring the meaning of a selected Tier II academic vocabulary word. Discuss the meaning of the word. Ask students to use the word in context. Provide examples of how the word can be used in a sentence. Figure 2.4 illustrates an example for the word *structure*.

Figure 2.4 Read Around the Word

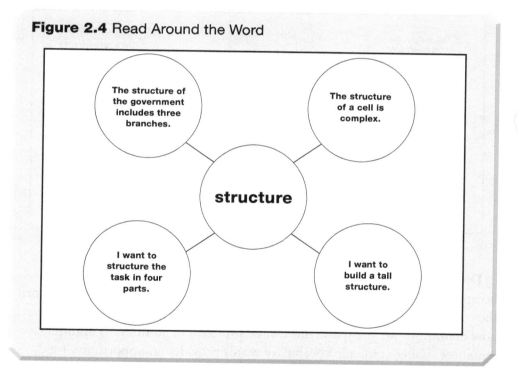

Talk about what the word means in each sentence, and then go on to ask students for synonyms of the selected word.

After providing some synonyms, ask students to use the synonyms in a sentence. Once the synonyms are in sentences, begin to have thoughtful discussions about the use of those words. For each sentence, talk about whether the word used can be substituted for the synonym. Why or why not? Is there a subtle nuance the synonym carries that makes it different from the word being used? If there is a subtle meaning, make note of it next to the synonym. Spend time talking about each sentence and whether the synonym can be used in each sentence properly. This strategy doesn't require you to create four branches out from the selected word; it can be two to four branches. Figure 2.5 shows a completed Read Around the Word for the word *structure*. The important thing about this strategy is the conversations that happen when you discuss the proper use of the words in context.

Figure 2.5 Completed Read Around the Word for *structure*, started in Figure 2.4

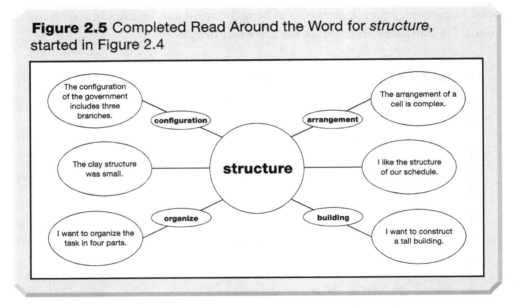

Differentiation: Read Around the Word can be difficult for students because they may not be used to using the synonyms in context. As a support, they can look up words in dictionaries or online. Figure 2.6 (page 49) shows how definitions for the synonyms can be provided in addition to example sentences. Using academic vocabulary words provides an opportunity for students to reference cognates from their primary languages. Many cognates are derived from conceptual academic vocabulary words. At any time, if a word has a cognate, point it out and ask students if the word they are studying sounds or looks familiar to a word they may know in another language. Challenge students to work in teams and assign each team a word from a vocabulary list to do Read Around the Word. Each table group is then expected to teach their word to the class.

Figure 2.6 Read Around the Word for *happy*

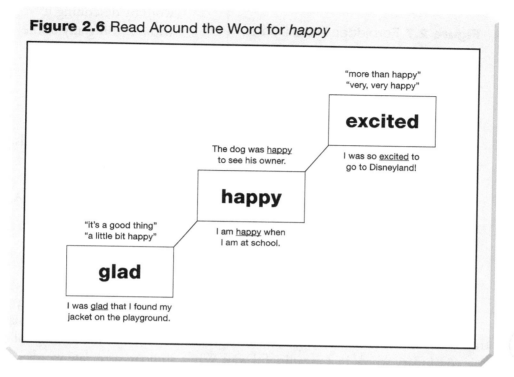

Forbidden Words

Purpose: Forbidden Words is a concept borrowed from the popular game Taboo. The purpose of the game in this context is to give students a chance to practice the meanings of the words they are studying by creating game pieces that identify the most common words associated with the words at hand. Forbidden Words provides students with a new method of looking at words from the traditional definition. It asks them to think about word associations. It helps students process and ensure they understand the meanings of words by thinking about how the words relate to other words. This strategy can be used with both academic and discipline-specific (content) vocabulary words.

Process: Use a vocabulary word list for this activity. Provide students with index cards. At the top of each index card, have students write their vocabulary words, making sure they write one word per card. Tell students to write five words on each card that are associated with the vocabulary word at the top of the card. Challenge students to include the most common words they think people would associate with the key word. The game is played as students quiz one another on the words. They have to get their partners to guess the vocab

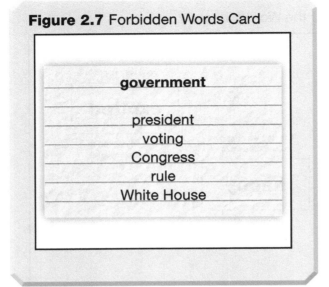

Figure 2.7 Forbidden Words Card

government

president
voting
Congress
rule
White House

word by describing it without using any of the words on the card. This challenges the class to have to think of other ways to explain the meaning of the word. And by creating the cards, students practice and review the meaning of their vocabulary words. A sample card is shown in Figure 2.7.

Differentiation: This game is pretty straightforward; creating the cards is the key to this strategy. As students create the game cards, they are reviewing the meanings of their vocabulary words in a meaningful way. When students associate words with other words, they demonstrate comprehension. For English learners at earlier levels of second language acquisition, it might help to give them more time with the words and have them work with partners to create the game cards. They can take the cards home to practice before using them in class to play the game.

Connect 3

Purpose: The main purpose of Connect 3 is to find the key concepts or ideas that connect words together. When students are asked to conceptualize how words are connected, it gives words purpose. Students gain a better understanding of the meaning of words when they see how words connect together. This strategy can be used with academic or discipline-specific (content) vocabulary words.

Process: Provide students with index cards. Using the vocabulary words, ask students to write one vocabulary word on the front of each card. Have students write three things that are associated with or part of their vocabulary words. After students create the cards, have them quiz their classmates by reading the three items they wrote on one side of the card and asking their classmates to guess the one word that connects the three words. An example is shown in Figure 2.8. This is a fun method of reviewing vocabulary words, both in creating the cards and playing the game.

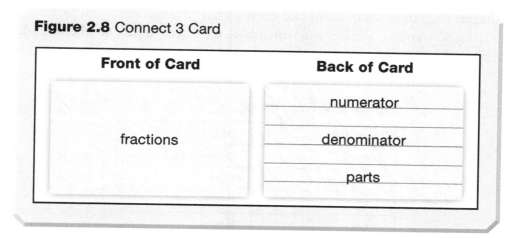

Figure 2.8 Connect 3 Card

Front of Card	Back of Card
fractions	numerator
	denominator
	parts

Differentiation: As with the other vocabulary strategies noted, differentiation occurs in the way the games are played or how the cards are distributed. But the words themselves should not be changed because the purpose of the strategy is for students to learn new vocabulary words and expand their understanding and use of the words. To differentiate, have students create the cards with partners or in teams. Challenge students by having them create multiple cards for the same words. This process makes students find more associations and related ideas or concepts.

Word Pairs (I Have, Who Has)

Purpose: The purpose of this strategy is to have fun with words by finding word pairs, or words that go together. This strategy can be used with all types of vocabulary, including functional, academic, and discipline-specific words. The main goal is to have students see how words connect to support the meanings of the vocabulary words.

Process: Create a set of word cards that pairs words by meanings or relationships. Provide each student with one card. Once everyone has a card, ask students to walk around the classroom and find a word that connects to their word. They must find a word pair. As they walk around, they should say, "I have (word)… who has (a suggested word)?" The "I have, who has…" gives students a chance to think about the words they have and what words they think might connect. Then, as students hear one another, they will find their pairs. After they find their pairings, ask students to share with their partners what their word means and discuss what connects the words. After one rotation, collect, shuffle, and redistribute the words to play another round. Figure 2.9 provides an example of paired word lists.

Figure 2.9 Word Pairs

Mammal	Dolphin
Reptile	Chameleon
Amphibian	Frog
Fish	Salmon
Insect	Bee

Differentiation: This strategy can be a little challenging for students at early levels of second language acquisition. It helps to pair them up to work in teams to find their word pairs. Again, do not change the words in any way because the goal is to expand their vocabulary. Students like to challenge themselves sometimes by trying to find their pairings faster and faster. As a challenge, consider timing the class to see how quickly they can find their pairs.

Concept Blossoms

Purpose: The Concept Blossoms strategy is a favorite for students because it challenges them to explore their learning by connecting it to familiar concepts and contexts. Concept Blossoms can be used with any word type. Constructivist learning theories state that it is easier to learn and remember information if students can connect it to something familiar (Anderson 1994). Concept Blossoms start with vocabulary terms and grow to make connections to a wide range of ideas, topics, and concepts.

Process: Using selected vocabulary words, begin by choosing one word and writing it in the center of a sheet of chart paper. Ask students to think about words or ideas that connect with or relate to the word in the middle. For example, if the word in the middle was *fossils*, students could offer words related to fossils, such as *dinosaurs*, *bones*, or *old*. After students share their ideas, you will "grow" the word to the next level. Then, take each of the related words and grow those. For example, by using the word *dinosaurs*, ask students to share words or ideas related to dinosaurs. They might say *extinct*, *brontosaurus*, etc. Repeat this process with the words *bones* and *old*. Once that level is done, keep growing. Continue branching out related ideas from each new word students add. Figures 2.10 and 2.11 (pages 53–54) provide examples of how the words grow and "blossom" as students keep thinking about their learning by expanding it to connect to new and prior knowledge.

Figure 2.10 First Grade Concept Blossom: Community Workers

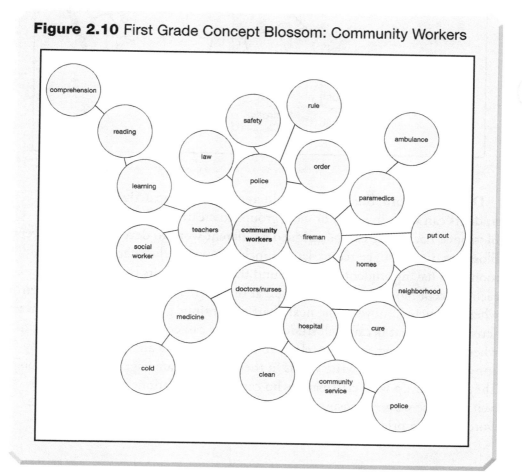

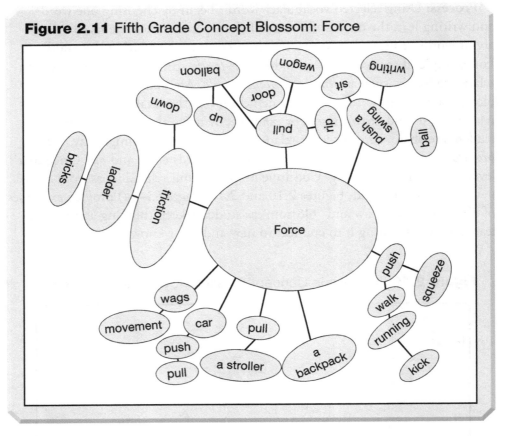

Figure 2.11 Fifth Grade Concept Blossom: Force

Differentiation: The task can begin as a whole-group activity, and then students can work in teams or table groups to create their own Concept Blossoms. Each table can be assigned a different word to develop their Concept Blossoms. Other suggested variations include putting the charts around the room and having students move around the room in pairs or groups to add to each concept blossom. Students begin at one poster, add their ideas, and then when instructed, move to the next chart to continue growing each word. These activities are great because all students feel they can contribute something when they add anything that relates to the words; there are no right or wrong answers. If newcomers write words in their primary language, that is okay too! They can pair up with classmates who can offer translations of the words as well. Because we are focusing on the concepts and the comprehension of the words, using a primary language is an appropriate scaffold.

Defining Academic Language in Context

Academic language, including functions, forms, and vocabulary (content and academic), can be captured in an "academic language bank." For years, we have used word banks and key vocabulary banks. An academic language bank captures the academic language that is core to the lesson. Once you are clear about your learning objective, content, thinking skill, resource, and product, you can determine your academic language bank. Figures 2.12–2.15 (pages 55–57) present a variety of academic language banks.

Language banks can be reused within and across disciplines each time the thinking skill resurfaces in a lesson. The vocabulary will change based on the content, but when a similar thinking skill is the focus of a lesson, the function and forms can be reused by including some vocabulary with the addition of new words based on the content and resource. For example, if we were comparing and contrasting two generals in the Civil War, I could provide students with access to the compare and contrast academic language bank. A week later, if we were comparing and contrasting two characters in a story, I could reuse the language bank by switching out some vocabulary.

Figure 2.12 Academic Language Bank (Compare and Contrast)

Students will be able to compare and contrast the Ancient Coliseum in Rome and the Los Angeles Coliseum.

- Function: Compare and Contrast
- Forms:

_____ is _____ but _____ is not.

_____ has _____ but _____ does not.

_____ can _____ however _____.

_____ can _____ whereas _____ cannot.

Though _____ can _____, _____ cannot.

It is clear that unlike _____, the _____ can _____.

Vocabulary	
Content	**Academic**
Coliseum	patterns
Rome	function
ruins	purposeful
ancient	significant
	demonstrate
	compare
	contrast

Figure 2.13 Academic Language Bank (Identify)

Language Features Task

- Function: Identify
- Forms:

It is a _____.

They are _____.

It shows _____.

I see _____.

It's _____.

Vocabulary	
Content	**Academic**
Coliseum	symbolic
Rome	identify
ruins	
ancient	

Figure 2.14 Academic Language Bank
(Defending and Stating a Claim)

Objective: Students will prove with evidence the main idea of _____ and write a brief literary response to defend their inference.

- Function: Defending and Stating a Claim
- Forms:

I think _____ was about _____

because _____.

_____ was about _____.

Based on _____, I can infer that

_____.

I deduce _____.

The main idea was _____. This was
evident in the text where it says

_____ .

According to _____, _____ was

really about _____.

Vocabulary (depends on selected text)	
Content	**Academic**
	deduce
	according to
	evident

Differentiating language banks is also helpful for students as they become more fluent in their academic language development. I recommend providing cue words as opposed to full sentence frames to help students' language to flow. Figure 2.15 shows a differentiated academic language bank.

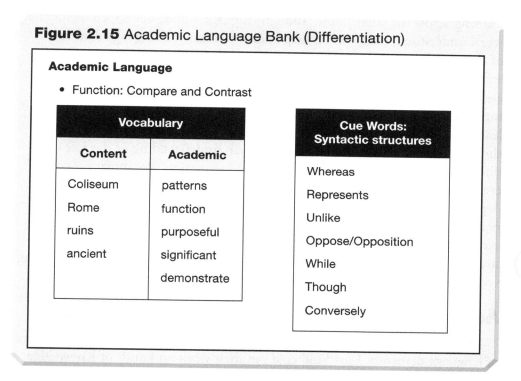

Figure 2.15 Academic Language Bank (Differentiation)

Academic Language

- Function: Compare and Contrast

Vocabulary		Cue Words: Syntactic structures
Content	**Academic**	
Coliseum	patterns	Whereas
Rome	function	Represents
ruins	purposeful	Unlike
ancient	significant	Oppose/Opposition
	demonstrate	While
		Though
		Conversely

Fluency

We should not lose sight of the fourth component of academic language, which is students' ability to use it with ease. *Fluency* will come with the opportunity for students to use functions, forms, and vocabulary frequently across the curriculum. We have all experienced language learning, whether through our families, at school, learning a foreign language, or to participate in new activities. These experiences clearly taught us that without the opportunity to use the language often, we lacked fluency and overall language development. For students, this is not an option. We might not have remembered what we learned in our high school Italian class, but our English learners must remember the English they are learning for academic success. To support this process, we must give students ample opportunities to use language. The chapters that follow present a wide range of comprehensible input and output strategies that can be used across the curriculum to help students practice using and accessing academic language for a variety of purposes.

Academic language development happens as students are immersed in learning across the curriculum. Though language will be developed incidentally when understood, teachers can help students access the language demands of their teaching and help them use language for academic purposes. To help students develop academic language, teachers must be able to identify the academic language for a lesson. This language will include the core functions, forms of language, and vocabulary needed to understand, access, and express learning. Teachers will be able to use core learning objectives to identify the functions, forms, and vocabulary with an understanding of the role of different tiers of vocabulary during content instruction. Vocabulary is part of every lesson; however, different levels or tiers of words take on different roles depending on the focus of the lesson. Understanding Beck and McKeown's tiering system is a start to understanding how teachers take up vocabulary across the curriculum. Once teachers know what words to focus on and how to engage students in a range of activities, they can guide students in acquiring vocabulary in ways to maximize understanding and retention.

Academic Language Beyond the Classroom

Families provide their children with diverse experiences that capture a range of language demands. Luis Moll et al., in their work on Funds of Knowledge (1992), share the rich knowledge base students develop by being active participants in their homes and communities. The experiences families provide for children range from the simplicity of talking to children to showing them some of the skills and practices involved with parents' or guardians' jobs both at home and at work.

I think back to the many funds of knowledge that I was exposed to as a child, and I am reminded that I came to school with lots of valuable knowledge and skills. My father is a mechanic and though his trade was fixing cars, he was able to take his knowledge base and apply it to fixing almost anything around the house. I would watch my father fix toasters, TVs, washing machines, stoves, faucets, and almost anything that needed repair. He would talk us through what he was doing and asked us questions to make sure we understood his processes. When I was 16, I complained about the squeaky brakes in my car and my father pulled me alongside him and talked me through changing the brake pads. I learned to listen and follow directions, problem solve, and figure out the right way to use tools and check my progress through constant monitoring. This was one of many examples of the funds of knowledge I was capturing at home and the complex language patterns I was gaining exposure to and processing.

There are so many examples of the rich language experiences I shared with my family. And even though they happened in Spanish, I was learning language patterns, cognitive processes, and concepts that I utilized at school when learning in English. These experiences provide students with not only funds of knowledge, but exposure to complex language as well. It is true that many of our out-of-school experiences can be more social, but there are plenty of complex language opportunities at home that also develop academic language (MacSwan and Rolstad 2003). The key is to capitalize on those rich language-learning experiences from home in school with the understanding that the focus of language development in school is academic in nature. Social language is a vehicle for communicating in school, but academic language is the vehicle for expressing formal learning across the curriculum: "If students don't know the academic language that affords them access to content, we do them a disservice" (Girard and Spycher 2007, 2).

Moment of Reflection

1. What academic language did you use in a recent lesson you presented? How did you provide students with access to the academic language?

2. How do you use academic and content (discipline-specific) vocabulary in your content-area lessons?

3. How can we use the distinction between Tier II and Tier III vocabulary to support students' overall academic language development?

4. What are the language experiences your students bring with them to the classroom?

5. How can you use the conceptual and concrete knowledge from students' homes and communities to inform your instruction?

Chapter 3

Differentiating for English Learners Across the Curriculum

Anticipation Guide

Decide whether you agree or disagree with the statements below.

- Only those students who are struggling need differentiation.

- All English language learners need the same support.

- Differentiation is about giving some students more work and some students less work.

A Road Map for Differentiation

The United States is a pluralistic society rich with diversity. Our classrooms are representative of this diversity. Diversity is an asset, and as teachers, we need to learn how to build on such assets. The range of learners from a wide variety of cultural, ethnic, linguistic, and academic backgrounds can also pose a challenge for teachers. Often, it feels overwhelming trying to determine the unique needs of each student, plan for differentiation, and implement lessons that address the diversity of the classroom. Teachers need to think about the collective needs of certain groups or look for patterns and similarities in terms of students' strengths and needs to accommodate learning in subsequent lessons.

English learners certainly have unique needs in the classroom, but we can also look at some collective needs based on what we know about how students learn a second language. We must utilize second language acquisition strategies that can support their learning at various levels of ELD. Figure 3.1 (pages 63–65) shows a range of supports for different levels of second language acquisition. This table is a starting point for general language supports used throughout the day. These instructional accommodations can be used intentionally during designated ELD to target the differing needs of ELs at specific levels of ELD. During integrated ELD, it may be a little more difficult as most teachers are working with a range of ELD levels in their classes. I encourage teachers to continue to use such strategies as they see fit, trying out those that may align with the instructional practices of the lesson as well as the general support for language development in general. However, I suggest a different approach when thinking about how to support English learners during integrated ELD. Often, when we think about what needs to be adjusted or differentiated, we are left to consider whether students met our learning objectives. This is one strategy for measuring the success of our lessons. Therefore, I take us back to the components of a comprehensive learning objective: content, thinking skills, resources, and products. A lesson is built upon these four elements that constitute a learning objective. When we think about differentiation, we can see the places in the lesson where students struggled and reflect on the factors that inhibited or impacted their ability to learn.

Every lesson we teach is based on content standards, which give us the content. Sometimes, the standards further share how we should approach and process the content; this is the thinking skill. For example, if the content focuses on characters, we would ask students to compare characters, identify characters, describe characters, etc. The thinking skill guides how we want students to cognitively interact with the content. Then, we need to think about the resources or materials we would use to give students access to the content and thinking. And there is always a product, whether oral or written, where students demonstrate their learning in some way. Resources and products might also be drawn from the standards; primary sources and drafting paragraphs, for example, are both present in the English language arts standards.

Figure 3.1 ELD Language Supports

ELD Level	
Emerging	• Teachers should develop a culture of risk and respect in the classroom—honor silence and encourage risk-taking with language.
	• Be sure to value students' native languages—encourage students to use their L1 as a scaffold to learning English.
	• Try to connect to prior knowledge and form connections between the content and their experiences.
	• Encourage students to use concrete visuals and realia.
	• Point and use nonverbal expression gestures to signal meaning.
	• Use sentence frames and complete sentences.
	• Use paragraph frames.
	• Demonstrate clear, precise language models.
	• Read aloud a range of informational and narrative texts.
	• Use graphic organizers with language supports.
	• Avoid using a lot of figurative language without explanation.
	• Use precise vocabulary with apposition (define in context when used).
	• Use cognates—words with similar pronunciation, spelling, meaning from a primary language to English.
	• Have students pair share.
	• Be sure to chunk content (oral and written)—stop and discuss frequently.
	• Encourage inquiry—through hands-on, minds-on experiences.
	• Provide opportunities for students to work with peers with similar needs and interact with a range of language levels.
	• Help students articulate key details and process big ideas.

Figure 3.1 ELD Language Supports *(cont.)*

ELD Level	
Expanding	<ul><li>Develop a culture of respect and rigor—expect students to use academic English for a range of experiences and demonstration of content knowledge.</li><li>Value their native language—make connections to English but expect the use of academic English.</li><li>Generate prior knowledge—build their knowledge base through exposure to more challenging, abstract content.</li><li>Use sentence frames—a wide range for common language functions.</li><li>Use a range of graphic organizers to demonstrate a variety of thinking processes.</li><li>Read aloud a range of texts.</li><li>Use multi-media—different perspectives and representations.</li><li>Introduce and explain figurative language.</li><li>Use a range of academic vocabulary words in context.</li><li>Chunk texts—pause and have students think, talk, and write frequently.</li><li>Encourage engaging and interactive inquiry.</li><li>Allow for small group work—explicitly teach group norms and processes toward independence.</li><li>Expect students to articulate big ideas and concepts supported with evidence.</li></ul>

Figure 3.1 ELD Language Supports *(cont.)*

ELD Level	
Bridging	<ul><li>Develop a culture of respect and academic rigor—expect high levels of content knowledge development and strong academic English.</li><li>Value their native language—celebrate their bilingualism, and expect the use of strong academic English.</li><li>Connect to prior knowledge—build a wide range of complex background knowledge.</li><li>Cue words for common language functions—limit full sentence frames.</li><li>Use self-generated and provided graphic organizers.</li><li>Use figurative language in context.</li><li>Use a range of vocabulary, such as similes, and explicitly discuss nuances.</li><li>Emphasize personal reading behaviors—note-taking, annotating text, and asking questions.</li><li>Encourage inquiry—verbalize a range of perspectives.</li><li>During small group work, have students take ownership of the work and interaction.</li><li>Expect students to articulate a range of big ideas and concepts for a text and explore content across sources as evidence to draw final conclusions.</li></ul>

Integrated approaches to teaching concentrate on selecting skills, resources, and products to support the learning of content. We can draw from English language arts and English language development standards to pair thinking skills, resources, products, and content to connect to a range of different content area topics and concepts. Let's look at a set of standards as an example.

Middle School NGSS (Next Generation Science Standards)

- MS-PS3-2 Energy: *Develop a model to describe that when the arrangement of objects interacting at a distance changes, different amounts of potential energy are stored in the system.*

Grade 7 CCSS ELA (Common Core State Standards English Language Arts)

- CSL.7.1: *Engage effectively in a range of collaborative discussions (one-on-one, in groups, and teacher-led) with diverse partners on grade 7 topics, texts, and issues, building on others' ideas and expressing their own clearly.*

ELD (English Language Development Standards)

- PI.7.BR.10b: *Write increasingly concise summaries of texts and experiences using complete sentences and key words (e.g., from notes or graphic organizers).*

Through an integrated approach, the standards help us see how we can ask students to develop a model to describe the scientific process outlined in the science standard by discussing their ideas with their peers (ELA standard) and then writing a summary about what they learned (ELD standard). Integrated approaches can help us find how to make language and literacy an ongoing part of all lessons.

Comprehensive learning objectives provide a clear road map for differentiation. After the lesson or during the lesson, you might think about which part of the lesson students struggled with: the content, the thinking skill, the resources, or the product. Each of these four elements can be differentiated to meet the needs of English learners. The sections that follow provide explanations of how to differentiate for each of the four elements. These are all entry points for differentiating for ELs.

Content

The focus in integrated ELD is teaching content. Language is learned and developed as part of the focus on content. Teachers learn to be intentional and explicit about language, but the main priority focuses on students learning the content. When we differentiate for content, we do not in any way change the content we expect students to learn. We maintain the same goal. We want to think about what students currently understand about the content and the prior knowledge they may bring to the learning experience. We also make assumptions about what we expect students to know prior to learning the content of our lessons. For example, if we were teaching multiplication concepts, we would expect students to come with knowledge of repeated addition. In language arts, if we were teaching character analysis, we would expect that students would already be able to describe characters and their actions, so they could then learn how to analyze them. The role of prior knowledge in this case is paramount in a student's access to the content and overall success with the lesson. To differentiate content, we want to start by thinking about the prior knowledge students may need to comprehend the content. Is the text or video presented to students in a way that expects them to bring certain knowledge or experiences so they can make meaning from the material? As an example, look at Figure 3.2 below.

Figure 3.2 Cave Painting

What is this image about? What is the core content/topic of the image? Now, think about the prior knowledge needed to make sense of the image. What knowledge is necessary to understand the main topic or idea of the picture? There is a broad range of different types of prior knowledge we may expect students to have to make sense of text or media. Figure 3.3 shows a broad range of prior knowledge we may need to consider and present to students before introducing our lessons.

Figure 3.3 Types of Prior Knowledge

Social-historical events

Vocabulary—meaning in context

Eras/time periods

Fashion

Economics

Social issues and acts

Architecture

Technology—evolution of, knowledge of, impact

Tools and their functions

Forms of communication

Companies and their purpose

Social-cultural norms

Historical-social-political figures

Laws, rights

Roles of people in society

Media

Pop culture

Differentiating content further includes scaffolding for students and helping them understand the broader context and relationships between content and concepts. Concept-definition maps help students learn content because they situate it in a broader context, helping students to better understand the information. Theories of learning in cognitive psychology help us appreciate that learning is easier when we can connect it to something familiar (Anderson 1977, 1994). Figure 3.4 below is an example of a concept-definition map.

Building background knowledge by identifying necessary prior knowledge for learning the content, as well as extending learning by contextualizing the content, will increase students' access to and retention of content.

Figure 3.4 Concept-Definition Map

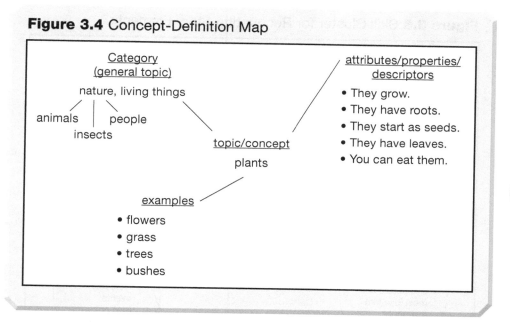

Thinking Skills

Deconstructing thought processes is one strategy for scaffolding thinking for English learners. Too often, we ask students to demonstrate thinking skills without teaching them explicitly how to think. We ask questions and prompt students to demonstrate comprehension of what they are learning. When students answer questions, they demonstrate their ability to successfully use thinking skills. But what happens when students can't answer the questions? What happens when the prompt and thinking process seem too complex at first? How do we scaffold thinking? How do we decide which skills students need help with to demonstrate the more complex thinking required for the task? In order to scaffold thinking, we need to think metacognitively about our thinking and *how* we think. If we ask students to infer an author's point of view, how do we explain the process of inferencing? What are the thinking processes we enact to successfully demonstrate this thinking skill? Without first thinking about the ways in which we arrive at our answers, we might struggle to scaffold it for students. A skill cluster helps capture our metacognitive processes by identifying a set of skills that are needed to demonstrate a more complex skill. Figures 3.5 and 3.6 (pages 70–71) provide examples of thinking skills clusters.

Figure 3.5 Skill Cluster for Recounting Story Elements

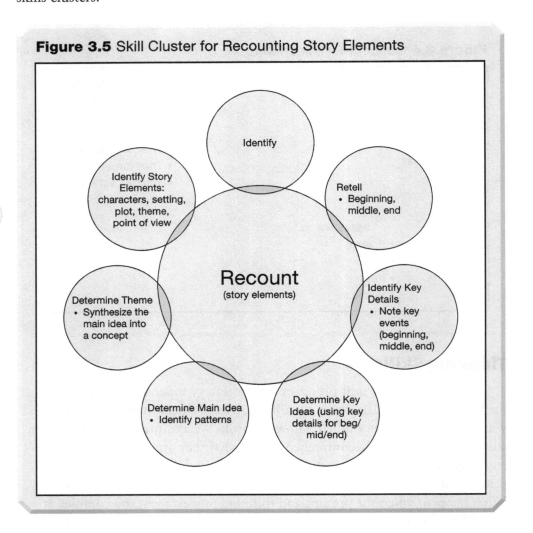

Figure 3.6 Skill Cluster for Inferencing

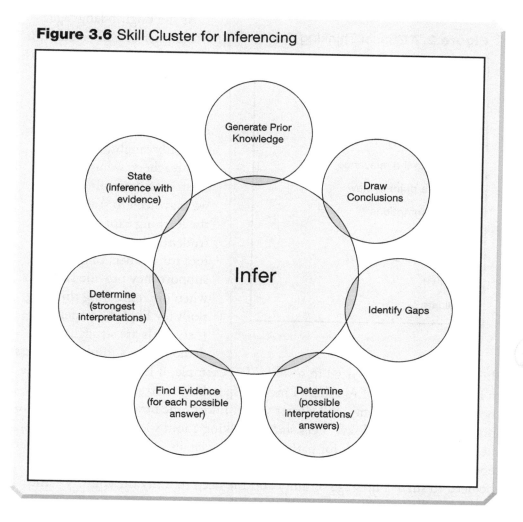

This is not an easy process because as teachers, we enact these skills naturally. We have had a lot of practice with them, and we are already complex thinkers. Stop and ask yourself, *how do I infer?* What do you cognitively do to infer the meaning of a text? Thinking about how you think can be tough at first. But you will find that you become more knowledgeable about how to scaffold the thinking skills required in your lessons. Figure 3.7 (page 72) shows some of the most common thinking skills students are expected to demonstrate as part of twenty-first century literacy skills. I encourage teachers to work together through these skill clusters for the core critical thinking skills to help one another prepare to scaffold thinking for students as needed.

Figure 3.7 Critical Thinking Skills

Prove with evidence

Judge with criteria

Relate

Note ambiguity

Determine the relevance

Defend a point of view

Note assumptions

Analyze

Compare and contrast

Recount

Evaluate

As the English language arts teacher or ELD teacher, I might spend a series of lessons teaching the thinking skills explicitly. Skills are part of the standards that need to be *taught*—not just assigned, but explicitly taught. As content-area teachers, we use skill clusters to determine where we may need to scaffold the learning experience for students. A skill cluster is a tool for teachers to guide the support they provide students when differentiating thinking skills for English learners. If students are struggling to demonstrate a thinking process about content, we may need to scaffold. For example, if I were to ask students to infer the message of Abraham Lincoln's speech at Gettysburg and I noticed they were struggling, my skill cluster would inform me how I might scaffold to move forward. I could say, "Let's start by talking about some key details from the speech, and then look for patterns in those details. What do the words that repeat mean to you? *We, we, we, we*—aha! *We* might infer that Lincoln saw the need to share a message of unity and the need to unify the country." The thinking skill cluster helped me think about where in the inference process I could go back to and build understanding so I could help my students get to the goal—to infer.

Skill clusters are not an exact science; thinking is complex, and the purpose of the cluster is for teachers to think through a process to get to the core thinking skill they want to teach. Teachers might go about the same thinking skill in different ways. As long as they are prepared to scaffold when needed, the skill cluster serves its purpose. I am often asked two things when it comes to skill clusters: Does it have to be developed in a cluster format, and do I show students the skill cluster? The skill cluster process encourages us to think deeply about our thinking. If the circles are not comfortable or preferred, you can write the steps out linearly. The purpose is to find the related skills you can call on when students may struggle to demonstrate the thinking skill you expect as the final objective of a lesson. Figure 3.8 lists the steps a fifth-grade ELA teacher recorded as her skill cluster to support her class in character analysis.

Figure 3.8 Example of a Linear Skill Cluster

Character Analysis

- Identify the main character.

- Describe the main character.

- Interpret the character's behaviors and relationships—what did they do? Why did they do it? What does it tell you about the character?

- Determine character traits.

- Prove with evidence—examples of the character demonstrating the trait.

- Draw conclusions—final thoughts about the character.

Students can definitely benefit from seeing metacognition on paper. However, the skill cluster is a practice for teachers to engage in as part of their planning process to scaffold thinking for students. With that said, I have seen teachers use the skill cluster process as a method of reviewing with students *how* they learned. Metacognition is a high-level thinking process, and we can show students what that looks like by reflecting after a lesson. For example, I observed a third-grade teacher discussing the process she went through with her class to compare and contrast the ecosystems they studied. Mrs. Machado started a quick discussion with the class to review the thinking process they used to compare and contrast. The script below is from Mrs. Machado's class, followed by a replica of the skill cluster chart (Figure 3.9, page 75) she created while reflecting with her class on how to make comparisons.

Teacher: *Let's look back at what we learned today. What did we focus on today?*

Students: *Ecosystems.*

Teacher: *Yes, but what was it that I asked you to do with ecosystems today?*

Students: *What animals live together in an ecosystem.*

Teacher: *Yes, but what did we do with that information?*

Students: *We filled out the Double Bubble.*

Teacher: *Right, and the Double Bubble is used to compare and contrast information. Let's talk about how we were able to compare and contrast. What did we do first?*

Students: *We wrote facts about the ecosystem.*

Teacher: *Right, we identified key details. What happened next?*

Students: *We circled the details that were about predators and prey.*

Teacher: *Good. We grouped the details together to form a variety of categories. We classified and categorized the details.*

Students: *Then we drew the lines to show how they are the same and different.*

Teacher: *Yes, then we looked for relationships by comparing and contrasting details about ecosystems. When you classify and categorize details, you can then look for the similarities and differences.*

Figure 3.9 Skill Cluster for Compare and Contrast

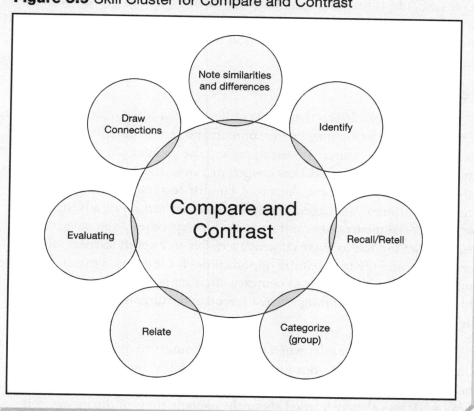

Mrs. Machado emphasized the academic language of the thinking skills and content to define the processes the class practiced. She went on to share that comparing and contrasting is a skill they use many times in all subject areas. In math, they might compare and contrast geometric figures; in history/ social science, they might compare and contrast ancient civilizations; and in English language arts, they might compare and contrast characters. The teacher made the point that now students can use their knowledge of the compare and contrast process for a variety of purposes.

As students become more fluent in their thinking, they will be able to use the skills naturally without having to think about the processes or struggle to demonstrate their thinking. Always keep in mind that differentiation may be needed. If students can demonstrate their thinking by the teacher simply telling them, "Let's compare and contrast two systems of the body we studied," and they can complete the given graphic organizer, then they don't need heavy scaffolds. If we notice that students are struggling to get started, then we should take a step back and guide them through the process. Skill clusters prepare us to scaffold thinking in a lesson while still maintaining the focus of the lesson—our content.

Resources

Another part of a lesson that can be differentiated is the resources. The focus of the integrated lesson may be the content, and standards drive the content we teach, but the resources we use to present the content can vary. Content can be presented through videos, images, pictures, drawings, diagrams, visuals, cartoons, trade books, peers, short text, familiar text, excerpts of text to preview in primary languages, multiple genres and text types, advertisements, websites, social media posts, and/or audio files (speeches). The range of resources we can use to make content accessible to English learners must be considered carefully to maximize opportunities for learning. Learning in a new language requires high levels of contextualized support. Students need to be able to access content through varied resources to support comprehension of the content.

Other factors to consider when selecting resources to differentiate for English learners include prior knowledge, readability, interest/engagement in the text type and content, and quality of the resource. If you begin thinking about what was already learned about the content/topic of the lesson, you should select a resource that builds on the knowledge students already have. The resource should also have a strong representation of the content. Is the information presented comprehensive enough to provide students with a range of details, facts, examples, and visuals to support students' learning of the content? Do we need to supplement the resource with other examples of the content, such as videos or pictures? Since content is the focus, it is helpful to consider the readability of selected resources. Students need to have exposure to high levels of academic language, so we should be sure to provide all students with access to the core text or resource.

However, if the text is too difficult for some students, supplemental materials, such as short texts, summaries with key points, or summaries in the student's primary language, might be provided. What I do not encourage is denying English learners access to the grade-level core resources because these materials provide strong examples of language they need to see frequently to continue their academic language development. The supplemental materials provide access to the content because language is best learned when students understand what they are learning. Comprehensible Input theory suggests that language can be learned only when it is understood (Krashen and Terrell 1983). Figure 3.10 captures considerations for resources when supporting English learners.

Figure 3.10 Considerations for Resources

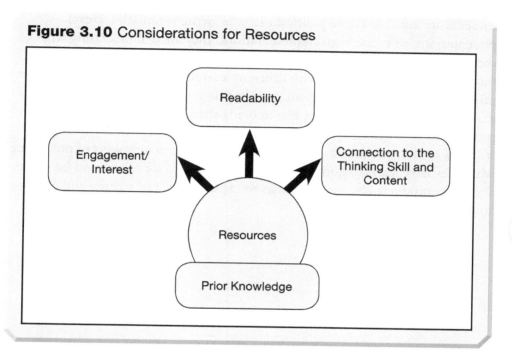

Products

Students need opportunities to share their learning through a wide range of products. Products can be defined as students' demonstrations of what they have learned, including oral and written products. Traditionally, students are asked to write essays and reports as they progress from elementary to middle and high school as methods of demonstrating their learning. These products are important because as students progress through school, these traditional forms of writing become the primary way of evaluating students' learning. If we think about our own experiences as we progressed through school, we wrote papers through high school and college, including college entrance exams requiring an essay. There are definitely explicit opportunities for students to present traditional products during designated ELD and English language arts. We will also use products across content areas, such as science, social studies, math, and a variety of elective classes. But we do not have to limit students' opportunities to demonstrate what they have learned to only written reports.

If the goal in integrated ELD is for students to demonstrate that they learned the content, they can do so through a range of products. Whether students are asked to create political cartoons, write summaries, create presentations, or create visual representations, they are demonstrating what they learned and understood. Providing a range of options for products can further help engage students with different learning preferences. Some students might like to use media to present their learning, other students might like to draw, and some students might like to orally share what they learned through presentations. Offering options throughout the year will not only re-engage students in all content areas, but give them exposure to new ways of presenting what they have learned. Some products may require a lot of text and language, and other products give opportunities to expand students' written and oral language practices and discourse.

Figure 3.11 provides examples of a range of products for ELs.

Figure 3.11 Concrete Products

Artistic Products	Performance Products	Written Products
Calligraphy	Advertisements	Articles
Cartoons	Athletic events	Autobiography
Charts	Book talks	Books
Collage	Comedy routines	Brochures
Computer graphics	Dance	Captions
Diagrams	Debates	Comic strips
Fashion design	Demonstrations	Ethnography
Jewelry	Guided tours	Journals
Mobiles	Mock trials	Laws
Murals	Musical performance	Pamphlets
Paintings	Poetry readings	Slogans
Photography	Puppet shows	Songs
Postcards	Reader's theater	
Posters	Reenactments	
Pottery	Skits	
Sculptures	Speeches	
Table settings	Storytelling	
Timelines	Theatrical performance	
Travel brochures	Vocal	
Videos	Weather reports	

Adapted from *Systems and Models for Developing Programs for the Gifted and Talented* (Renzulli and Gubbins 2009)

Note: There are also abstract products students can create to demonstrate understanding of concepts like empathy, persistence, and self-efficacy.

Differentiation can be difficult when we have a wide range of learners in our classrooms. Thinking about how to differentiate by looking at the elements that comprise a lesson can help us decide where and what to differentiate. Content, thinking skills, resources, and products can serve as a framework for differentiation to guide English learners in meeting content objectives. These four elements give us entry points to differentiation by helping us determine where or what about the lesson challenged students. Was the content too advanced? Did they need more prior knowledge or a broader context to connect to? Was the resource limiting? Was the thinking too complex; did they need scaffolding? Did the product help students demonstrate what they learned? These questions can help us target where or what in our lesson may need to be adjusted, supplemented, or enhanced to help English learners comprehend the content and demonstrate what they have learned.

Moment of Reflection

1. How can thinking skills be differentiated to support English learners? Always remember that we want to keep the expectations high and expect all kids to reach the required thinking skills in the end.

2. How are content, thinking skills, resources, and products connected? How do they inform one another to ensure a focused lesson with clear outcomes?

3. Think about a lesson you recently taught. What went well? What didn't go as well as you planned? Was the content or resources used too difficult, did the product not fit the task or students well, or was the thinking skill too advanced and needed to be scaffolded? Revisit your lesson and try to point out the area or need. How could you have taught it differently?

Part II: Comprehensible Input and Output Strategies

Chapter 4

Comprehensible Input

Anticipation Guide

Decide whether you agree or disagree with the statements below.

- Learning a new language requires that the content or message be understood in order for learning to occur.

- Strategies are an effective way to enhance comprehensible input.

- It is important to make connections between students' home and community experiences and school experiences.

Content and Language

One of the most common approaches to supporting ELs with language across the curriculum has been to focus on comprehensible input. *Comprehensible input*, a concept supported by the work of Stephen Krashen and Tracy Terrell (Input Comprehension Hypotheses), forwards the idea that if students are to develop language, they must understand the message/content being communicated (1983). With a strong focus on content in the disciplines, comprehensible input is at the forefront of integrated approaches to language instruction. It makes sense that if students are going to learn the content at hand, they must understand it. This includes the ability to learn language along the way. Krashen and Terrell argue that for language acquisition to occur, the message or the content being taught must be comprehensible. Comprehensible input serves a dual purpose, as English learners are learning content and language simultaneously.

Included in the hypothesis is the idea that learning can only occur if the language presented is slightly more advanced/complex than students' current language skill level. This resembles classical theories of learning by Lev Vygotsky (1978), including the idea that if learning is to occur, students need guidance with knowledge and skills just beyond what they can do independently. Vygotsky refers to the potential for learning between the known and the unknown as the Zone of Proximal Development. Vygotsky's Zone of Proximal Development explains that the potential to learn rests between what children can do on their own and the support they receive by a "more knowledgeable other" to achieve a learning goal or task (1978). The Zone of Proximal Development is similar to what Krashen and Terrell suggest for language learning. To learn language, the learning target must be slightly above what students can already do with language. This complexity will ensure comprehensible input. These theories have guided content-area teachers for decades, working to ensure that the content being taught is clearly understood by all students. For many years, Specially Designed Academic Instruction in English (SDAIE) strategies were developed and implemented to support comprehensible input. They are still used today and remain effective in supporting English learners.

The focus on comprehensible input remains strong in integrated ELD and we must continue to support teachers in making content accessible for English learners. If language is to be learned, the information must be understood. By using traditional and highly effective SDAIE strategies as well as new and innovative English language development strategies, teachers will continue to help all students learn and understand content. Comprehensible input strategies must be expansive enough to support the complexities of learning content that requires students to utilize a range of language and literacy skills. Teachers must scaffold thinking for English learners, make content "visible," and engage students with content. Comprehensible input includes a range of approaches with key elements to support student learning, generate prior knowledge, and provide students access to content.

Accessing Prior Knowledge and Building Background

Traditional approaches to prior knowledge have been discussed in Chapter 3 as a method of differentiating content for English learners. Depending on the content to be studied, it is important to know what your students already know and understand about the content and build upon their prior knowledge. To make content comprehensible, it helps to connect new learning to existing schema (our current knowledge base). Schema theory (Anderson 1977, 1994) posits that if we can connect new learning to existing schema, something familiar, it makes the learning experience easier. For example, if students were beginning to study circuits in science, we could start by talking about their knowledge of electricity and how it is used in their day-to-day lives. This discussion helps students find authentic connections and draw from something familiar before learning such a complex concept as circuits. This is not a new idea; we use pre-reading strategies to help students access text regularly. We use these strategies by asking students what they already know about a topic, showing images or visuals of related content to the topic at hand, showing videos or providing some preview texts that overview the topics, encouraging students to ask questions about what they will be learning, and reviewing what has already been learned. What I want to challenge us to think about are new ways of building bridges for students. We access prior knowledge and connect with students based on content, but we can further make learning authentic and comprehensible by connecting to students' primary language learning experiences and the skills they have from their own home and community experiences.

Connecting to Students' Experiences

Academic language is often referred to as the language of school; however, students are exposed to diverse experiences in their worlds outside of school that include higher-level thinking processes. Work by Henry Jenkins (2009) on participatory cultures helps us see the range of complex skills that children are involved in by participating in a variety of social contexts both face-to-face and virtually. Jenkins identifies eleven participatory culture skills. These skills are enacted by students naturally as they interact with knowledge and other people through informal and formal communication structures. Figure 4.1 (page 86) outlines the participatory culture skills. These skills are already part of students' worlds.

Figure 4.1 Participatory Culture Skills

Play	the capacity to experiment with one's surroundings as a form of problem-solving
Performance	the ability to adopt alternative identities for the purpose of improvisation and discovery
Simulation	the ability to interpret and construct dynamic models of real-world processes
Appropriation	the ability to meaningfully sample and remix media content
Multitasking	the ability to scan one's environment and shift focus as needed to salient details
Distributed Cognition	the ability to interact meaningfully with tools that expand mental capacities
Collective Intelligence	the ability to pool knowledge and compare notes with others toward a common goal
Judgment	the ability to evaluate the reliability and credibility of different information sources
Transmedia Navigation	the ability to follow the flow of stories and information across multiple modalities
Networking	the ability to search for, synthesize, and disseminate information
Negotiation	the ability to travel across diverse communities, discerning and respecting multiple perspectives, and grasping and following alternative norms

Jenkins argues that each of these skills has a role in a child's formal education in the classroom. All content areas have the potential to engage students in experiences that utilize participatory culture skills. These experiences are already part of many activities in the classroom without our conscious understanding of the skills students are utilizing. As students use skills, they interact with language. Language is used to access information, interpret information, and produce a range of written and oral language forms. Academic language does not only exist in schools and within school contexts. As Jenkins shows us, the complexities of students' interactions beyond the classroom further expose them to academic language.

When students are asked to utilize complex thinking skills, they are exposed to complex language. A child's world is rich with diverse language experiences. We need to broaden our understanding of academic language to see it as language for exploring, producing, and explaining complex thinking processes, and those can happen inside and outside of school. Students are living in a world full of access to knowledge and language. They exist in social spaces that are rich with discourse and complex thinking. To help students with comprehensible input, we can build bridges between what they know and the experiences they engage in within the classroom. Figure 4.2 (pages 87–89) shows examples of the many ways students develop participatory culture skills and ways we ask students to use these skills in the classroom.

Figure 4.2 Participatory Culture Skills Classroom Connections

Play	Kahoot
	Science experiments
	Plays/drama
	Quizzes
	Labs
	Padlet
	Conflict resolution activities (role playing real world scenarios)
	Analyzing news sources
Performance	Acting out a historical scenario
	Create a theoretical historical situation
	Reader's theatre
Simulation	Simulated history journal—day in the life of a soldier
	Reader response journals—if you were (character) what would you do?

Figure 4.2 Participatory Culture Skills Classroom Connections *(cont.)*

Appropriation	Research reports Presentations Infographics Outsides sources Blending sources
Multitasking	Google Classroom Flip grids Padlet Music while working Layered activities Work stations/center Literature circles Note-taking
Distributed Cognition	Interacting with technology in the classroom Labs Primary source documents Published writing (typed)
Collective Intelligence	Group work Projects Table talk Pair share Debate teams
Judgment	Verify sources Class discussions Presentations—peer feedback

Figure 4.2 Participatory Culture Skills Classroom Connections *(cont.)*

Transmedia Navigation	Google Hangouts with scientist Google Expeditions (virtual field trips) Media scavenger hunt Utilize different links for research
Networking	Research papers Projects Interviews Team sports—physical education Publishing writing—multiple formats
Negotiation	Group presentations Labs Book clubs

Making connections explicit helps students build bridges for learning. For example, when students are tasked with completing research papers, they do not always realize that they already have and use the skills they need at home or with their friends. Remind students that when they create memes to send to their friends, they are searching and looking for the right image as well as the right words or texts to put it together. This process takes research. When students create worlds in Roblox and try to win by joining teams in each others' worlds, they use negotiation—just like when they decide what the main characters in their fictional narratives will be like and what adventures they will engage in. Drawing from the familiar makes the content and learning experience more comprehensible.

Use of Tools and Resources

Teachers further draw from a range of tools and resources to facilitate comprehensible input. These can include teacher supports, concrete tools, and strategies. Figure 4.3 (pages 90–91) provides a range of ideas for helping students access content to increase comprehensible input and language learning.

Figure 4.3 Supporting Comprehensible Input

Teacher Supports	Teacher monitoring (proximity)
	Repeated phrases
	Establish routines—familiar language
	Objectives written on the board
	Deconstruct the objective
	State and restate the objective before, during, and after the lesson
	Listen-Guide-Prompt-Recast
	Provide a road map for the lesson/day
	Connect previous learning to new learning
	Make real-world connections
	Ask a range of questions
	Speak clearly with expression and appropriate tone
	Provide wait time
	Have students add to notes after pair shares
	Deconstruct prompts/questions
	Provide cognates
	Opportunities for reflection
	Quick writes
	Intentional walking—consistent movement and monitoring student learning
	Encourage the use of complete sentences and academic language
	Modeling: how to listen, note-taking, writing
	Provide visible access to text (document cameras or individual copies)
	Provide multiple opportunities for talk
	Model and use academic vocabulary: identify it, explain it, and discuss it
	Clarify vocabulary with familiar language
	Connect to students' personal experiences
	Offer support when students struggle

Figure 4.3 Supporting Comprehensible Input *(cont.)*

Concrete Tools	Graphic organizers
	Anchor charts with visuals and examples
	Sentence frames
	Journals—to record thinking and learning (low stakes)
	Notebooks—organized by content, processes, vocabulary
	Completed models
Strategies	Pair shares
	Table talk
	Group work—explicit directions (roles and expectations)
	Range of SDAIE strategies

Many of the suggestions in the table may be familiar, as we have used so many of these to support English learners during content-area instruction. Though all the ideas listed are equally important to provide comprehensive support for ELs, a few favorites include deconstructing objectives, intentional walking, and listen-guide-prompt-recast.

Deconstructing Objectives

Learning objectives provide teachers and students with clear expectations for learning. The objective tells students what they will learn to help narrow their focus, and it reminds teachers what the goal is for the lesson. Teachers can measure what students have learned by assessing how students are able to meet the objective at the end of the lesson. To support English learners with content learning, there are a few ways to use objectives intentionally. Begin by establishing a clear objective. Chapter 3 on differentiation reminds us of the four core elements of an objective: content, thinking skills, resources, and products.

Once we have our objective, we should begin a lesson by presenting the objective to the class. Presenting the objective should be done both orally and in writing. To make sure students understand the objective, it helps to deconstruct it with the class. For example, point out the content and note it in some way: highlight it, underline it, place a box around it, or circle it. Then, revisit the thinking skill and remind students that they will explore the content through the thinking skill identified. Again, call it out with some notation that is different from what was used for the content. Continue to deconstruct the objective by calling out and noting the resource that will be used and the product students will create in the end. If applicable, show an example of the product or point to sentence frames or language cues students might use to complete the product. If any of the words reviewed in the objective have cognates, write them above the words to help bridge language and concept connections. Figure 4.4 shows an example of a learning objective that has been deconstructed with a class.

Objective: SWBAT (Students will be able to)/(I will) compare and contrast two characters in the text, "Recess Queen," and complete a Double Bubble map.

What is different?	(C) Content
What is similar or alike?	(R) Resource
(T/S) Thinking Skill	(P) Product

Figure 4.4 Deconstructed Learning Objective

Objective:

What is similar or alike? (T/S) What is different?

SWBAT (I will) <u>Compare and Contrast</u>

(C)   (R)

two <u>characters</u> in the text, <u>Recess Queen</u>

(P)   Literature, fictional story

and complete a <u>Double Bubble map</u>.

(T/S)-Thinking Skill, (C)-Content, (R)-Resource, (P) Product

This process should only take a few minutes. As the lesson continues, when students make great strides to meet the objective, you can point it out during the lesson by reminding them what the learning objective is. Once the lesson is over, revisit the objective, and provide students with a moment of reflection. Ask them to think about what they learned and how they know they met the objective.

Intentional Walking

Intentional walking is powerful. When we monitor student learning, we are able to informally assess students and make instructional decisions in the moment to guide student learning. Walking around the classroom is the first step toward intentional walking. This seems obvious, but I have been in hundreds of classrooms where teachers watch from the front of the classroom or at their desks while students work and learn. We need to walk around to see, listen, and learn about what students are learning. Active observation helps us grasp how students make sense of the lesson and work toward meeting the learning objective. Consider what to look and listen for when monitoring learning. This is why our learning objectives are so important. As we walk around, we want to look for evidence that students are learning what we expected—the objective. For example, while walking, stop and listen to students talking. Ask them clarifying questions, probe their thinking, question their ideas, encourage their use of academic language, and ask them to summarize key points from their group work. Intentional walking further provides opportunities to support students' language development. When talking with students, you can help them articulate their ideas by recasting or orally offering suggestions for how to explain their thinking through academic language. As simple as this teacher support may seem, it is a powerful tool to guide student learning of content and to develop language.

Listen-Guide-Prompt-Recast

Integrated ELD provides additional challenges for English learners. In integrated ELD, English learners are typically mixed with students who have developed a range of English language abilities along with English-dominant students. This can pose a challenge for English learners to have the confidence to use English to participate during integrated ELD. Krashen and Terrell further present the Affective Filter Hypothesis (1983), which purports that in order for language to be learned, students need to feel safe taking risks with language. Learning new content is already a challenge, and when that is coupled with learning language at the same time, it can make a student feel intimidated and less likely to participate. Without participation (i.e., practicing the language), the ability to develop fluency with academic language is impacted. We need to establish safe spaces in our classrooms for English learners to make mistakes and continue to improve their academic English.

Encouraging students to try out language should be coupled with explicit guidance and support for producing academic language. Make sure to *listen* patiently as ELs try to express their learning, and *guide* their ideas by asking them to restate their thoughts or point to evidence or resources that helped them form their ideas. Use this information gained from the student to *prompt* their learning. Ask them questions to get them to think more deeply and use more language to express their ideas. Prompting can come in the form of clarifying questions for students who are developing summarizing skills or questions to extend thinking, such as: *How did you know? What made you think that? What evidence do you have? Are there other alternatives?* As English learners work to express their ideas, this is an opportunity to *recast* their ideas for them in complete sentences that model academic language. Recasting is repeating what students say through more formal academic registers and vocabulary. This process helps validate students' ideas and further provides access to academic language models.

Making Text Comprehensible

A challenge for English learners during content-area instruction is the amount of written language they encounter. Both traditional and non-traditional texts, such as media-based references, are rich with academic language and require scaffolding to access and interpret. Deconstructing texts with students helps them understand the information and construct their own understanding. A wide range of strategies can be used to guide students' access to text, including anticipation guides, Main Idea Tree, Say-Mean-Matter, Somebody-Wanted-But-So-Then, and Zooming-In, Zooming-Out.

Anticipation Guides

Purpose: Anticipation guides are a great way to access prior knowledge and prepare students for the core content/concepts of the lesson. This strategy further challenges students to use the language of opinion and argumentation to take a position and defend it.

Process: Look at the core content that your lesson will be covering. Select a concept that connects to a big idea, which encourages students to take a position on it. A big idea is a statement that expresses an idea, a position, or a point of view. For example, a big idea could be the study of relationships between plants and animals in an ecosystem. You might think of a concept it fits within, such as associations or interdependence. From this concept, create a statement that can be argued. For example, *Do all relationships require that each member participate equally? Are all relationships purposeful? Can one member of a relationship need more help than another? Is interdependence always equal in effort and need?*

The anticipation guide presents questions that students can answer with *yes* or *no*. The questions give them something to talk about. Figure 4.5 is an example of an anticipation guide. Students simply mark *yes* or *no* for each question if they agree or disagree. Students then engage in a conversation about what they selected. They can share with partners, as a table group, or as a class. The anticipation guide helps students connect with broader concepts, which helps them learn the details and content during the lesson.

Figure 4.5 Anticipation Guide

	Yes	No
Do all relationships require that each member participate equally?		
Are all relationships purposeful?		
Can one member of a relationship need more help than another?		
Is interdependence always equal in effort and need?		

Differentiation: Anticipation guides are great tools for English language learners because they help ELs make conceptual connections. Being able to connect learning to known concepts learned in any language helps ELs connect to the new learning in English. As noted in Chapter 1, English learners develop conceptual understandings when they learn in any language.

For example, the concept of relationships is something they could have learned about in their primary language. They don't have to relearn the concept; they can connect the new English term with what they already know about relationships. For students with primary languages that are Latin/Greek-based, there are several cognates they can connect to. Conceptual words are more likely to have cognates than concrete terms. In this case, the words *relationship* and *participate* have cognates in other languages, such as Spanish—*relaciones* and *participar*. Therefore, adding cognates into the anticipation guide is an excellent method of differentiation for learners.

Main Idea Tree

Purpose: The Main Idea Tree is a great method to show students how we can move from details to main ideas that are supported with evidence all in one strategy. The purpose of a main idea tree is to guide students from the details of what they are reading to seeing the relationship between those details to determine the main point of the text. It is an after-reading strategy, as students will need to gather details to draw conclusions. The Main Idea Tree is best used with informational texts or audio-visual materials.

Process: After reading or viewing a chapter or segment of a text or video, pause to ask students to recall the key details from the text or video. Record their ideas on the top of the tree. Their ideas symbolize above the surface as basic recall details. From there, ask students to look at the details closely and look for any patterns, words, or ideas that repeat to identify the topic of the text or video. Write the topic in the trunk of the tree. Once you have a topic, students are then positioned to determine the main idea. Ask students what point, argument, or idea the author is trying to make. From here, students will explore possible main ideas. Add the main idea to the base of the trunk, as they are now going under the surface to get to the deeper meaning. From there, we always want students to prove their ideas by providing evidence to show their thinking. Look back at the details and ask students which ones best support their main idea. Record those in the roots of the tree. The Main Idea Tree visually shows students how to move from details, to topics, to main ideas with evidence. Figure 4.6 (page 97) is an example of a Main Idea Tree for the book *Plants,* a first-grade informational text.

Figure 4.6 Main Idea Tree

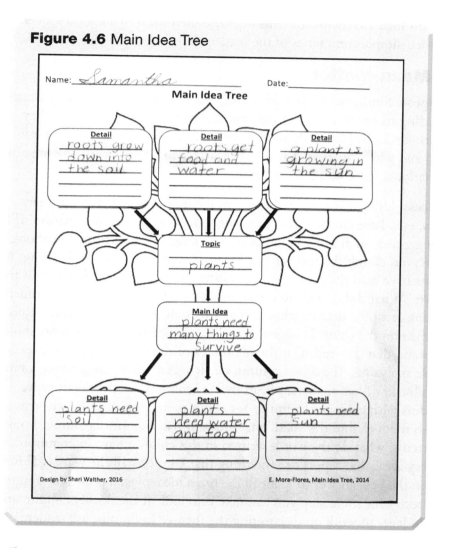

Name: *Samantha*   Date:_____

Main Idea Tree

Detail
roots grow down into the soil

Detail
roots get food and water

Detail
a plant is growing in the sun

Topic
plants

Main Idea
plants need many things to survive

Detail
plants need soil

Detail
plants need water and food

Detail
plants need sun

Design by Shari Walther, 2016   E. Mora-Flores, Main Idea Tree, 2014

Differentiation: Main Idea Trees are a great way for English learners to *visibly* see where ideas come from. They will be able to track their thinking by working their way down the tree. It is also helpful because they are guided through the process of deconstructing the text from its details to its main ideas. As an extension, you can further have each student use the information to write a paragraph that summarizes the text/video. For example, using the Main Idea Tree for *Plants*, the student might write from the middle of the tree down: *The book was about plants. Plants need many things to survive. Plants need sunshine, rich soil, and water. Some plants also need a lot of space to survive.*

The Main Idea Tree helps students organize their ideas in a logical sequence to write their simple summaries of the text.

Say-Mean-Matter

Purpose: Similar to a Main Idea Tree, Say-Mean-Matter is a great strategy for guiding students to move from the facts to the big ideas of what they are learning. In Say-Mean-Matter, students discuss what they see, what it means, and why it matters. Say-Mean-Matter can be used with any literature, informational texts, or audio-visual materials.

Process: Using any source of content, including texts, videos, primary sources, etc., have students first read, view, or listen to the information. If it is a longer text, such as a chapter book or a long selection from a textbook, students can chunk the text for Say-Mean-Matter by chapter or heading. After students have read the text, begin by asking them to note the key details from the text: "What did it say?" Record their ideas on a chart. Then, ask students, "Looking at all the details, what do you think all these details mean?" Record their ideas on the chart. I suggest recording a range of ideas. Students should understand that the "mean" is the main idea of the text or part of the text they are analyzing. The *Mean* column challenges students to generate a range of possible key ideas that stem from the *Say* column. Students can prove their ideas with evidence from the *Say* column, making their "mean" true. To push them to find the "best" main idea, revisit the *Mean* column. Look for patterns; what do the words written in this column have in common? Are there key ideas that repeat or something that connects all the words? This will give you the best answer to identify the main idea, overall point, or argument of the text. One more step you can take is to look at the *Matter* column and push students to work on discovering the theme. To do this, ask students to look at the *Matter* column and to think about one or two words that capture what the column is all about. For example, in the Say-Mean-Matter example (Figure 4.7, page 99), the *Matter* column is possibly about adapting. In the second example (Figure 4.8, page 99), the *Matter* column can be conceptualized as the theme of trustworthiness or honesty.

Figure 4.7 Say-Mean-Matter, Kindergarten, Science/Weather unit

Say/See	Mean	Matter
Kids playing Kids throwing snowballs A snowman Kids wearing scarves, hats, gloves, books Snow is falling.	It's cold. It's winter.	It's important to know the weather so you can decide what to wear and play.

Figure 4.8 Say-Mean-Matter, 3rd Grade, *Tricky Monkey*

Say/See	Mean	Matter
There is a monkey. He is a liar. He played tricks. He saved the monkeys from the leopard. They forgave the monkey. There is a concerned aunt. He likes to get attention.	If you are a known liar, no one will believe you. People won't trust you if you lie all the time. If you are bored, you need to make better choices to entertain yourself. You can get attention in a positive way.	You want to be a trustworthy person so people will trust you. If you lie all the time, people won't want to be your friend. If you do make a bad choice in life, you should try to repair it or get their trust back.

Differentiation: Say-Mean-Matter can further be used with visuals or videos. Students can analyze a visual and discuss what they see, what it means, and why it matters. The kindergarten Say-Mean-Matter example above was completed as part of a science unit on weather. The teacher showed different pictures of children playing during different times of the year. As with the Main Idea Tree, Say-Mean-Matter helps guide English learners to work from details toward main ideas and in this case, to further make meaning from their learning. Deconstructing the text or video by looking at it in chunks and moving across the table helps students process the information. And for all students, making meaning of their learning by seeing the relevance of what they learn can help them remember the details of what they learn. Encourage students, especially as they are becoming more proficient in English, to do another level of analysis. Look at all the possibilities everyone came up with in the *Mean* column and see if students can find patterns in the ideas to find the main idea of the text. They can also look at the *Matter* column and look for patterns there to find a theme. The theme captures the conceptual base of the text. Teachers can tell students to think about one word or phrase that best captures the ideas in the *Matter* column. For example, the Say-Mean-Matter by third graders on *Tricky Monkey* has some key ideas in the *Matter* column that can be examples of themes such as friendship, trustworthiness, or honesty. Once students move to these levels of analysis, they can use the Say-Mean-Matter chart to write a summary of the text.

Somebody-Wanted-But-So-Then

Purpose: Somebody-Wanted-But-So-Then is a simple method of teaching students how to summarize narrative text. This strategy provides a concrete summary of the text, which means it does not analyze the text for a main idea or theme as part of the summary. Summaries that include the reader's interpretation of the text's thesis/main idea would be abstract summaries. This strategy helps students to synthesize the text and focus on the core events to successfully summarize.

Process: The name of the strategy guides the process. Following the words—*somebody, wanted, but, so,* and *then*—will set up how to process the text. After reading a narrative, start by asking students, who is the text about? The main character is the *somebody*. For example, after reading the story of the three little pigs, students might identify the wolf as the main character. Then, proceed from there: *The Wolf wanted to…* Ask students to add the next piece. *The Wolf wanted to eat the pigs…* Then say, "But what happened?" *The wolf wanted to eat the pigs, but he couldn't catch them…* Now, direct them to how the character tried to solve the problem: "So, what did he do?" *The wolf wanted to eat the pigs, but he couldn't catch them, so he chased them from house to house, huffing and puffing.* "Then, what happened as a result of his efforts?" *The wolf wanted to eat the pigs, but he couldn't catch them, so he chased them from house to house, huffing and puffing and blowing their houses down. Then, he gave up because the last house was made of bricks.* Using the language of the strategy helps guide your questions as you scaffold the summary with students. Figure 4.9 (page 101) demonstrates the strategy used with a nonfiction text.

Figure 4.9 Somebody-Wanted-But-So-Then for Nonfiction Text

Somebody	Wanted	But	So	Then
Kids from all over the country and Mexico and Jamaica	to participate in and win the national spelling bee	not everyone can win	they have to study very hard and pore over words for hours	one day they may win the spelling bee

Kids from all over the country and Mexico and Jamaica wanted to participate in and win the national spelling bee, but not everyone can win, so they have to study very hard and pore over words for hours, so one day they may win the spelling bee.

Differentiation: This strategy provides language cues to guide English learners' summaries. It is a simple method for them to use the language to capture the core elements of the story they read. The words from the strategy set up a sentence frame for students to use to articulate their summaries. Advanced English learners can stretch each part of the summary by creating a sentence for each part. This will help them learn to extend their language to express their learning.

Zooming-In, Zooming-Out

Purpose: Zooming-In, Zooming-Out is a strategy that can be used with students after they read or view content to help them move from details to real-world connections. This strategy is best used with informational text or videos. As part of the strategy, teachers start by guiding students to look closely at details in the text/video and then at the bigger concepts associated with the content. This process helps students make connections beyond the text/video to other topics or content they have studied or are familiar with. In the end, students get a chance to draw final conclusions with a summary statement to capture their learning. It helps students see how content is connected and shows the importance of looking at the bigger concepts and ideas that frame their learning. It is easier to remember details if they can be embedded in big ideas and connected across disciplines.

Process: After reading the text, begin by asking students to identify the topic of the reading. Then, ask students to write a list of important details they heard or read from the text. I like to use small sticky notes for this part because students will be sharing their ideas with one another and sorting them. When using sticky notes, ask students to use one per detail. Once the details have been gathered, have students work with partners to combine their sticky notes and sort them between what they would agree are the most important and least important details. The sorting process helps students focus on key details. Have them place their final sticky notes on their Zooming-In, Zooming-Out templates, remembering to place the sticky notes under the appropriate columns, *Most Important* or *Least Important* details. The next step is to think about things that are *similar to* the main topic. What other topics or concepts serve a similar purpose or are similar to the topic in some way? These questions help students form associations and create mental concept maps about the topic at hand. The fourth step is to talk about what they can think of that is *related to* the topic. I often ask students to think of the following when deciding what is related to the topic: "You can't have (topic) without _____." To make sure students are gaining a deep understanding of the topic, the next step is to determine some "non-examples." Have students brainstorm what they know of that is not associated with or is just not an example of the topic at hand. The final step is to take their overall understanding of the topic based on all the steps and write a final summative statement(s) about the topic. Figure 4.10 (page 103) shows a completed Zooming-In, Zooming-Out based on an article about the history of radio.

Figure 4.10 Zooming-In, Zooming-Out

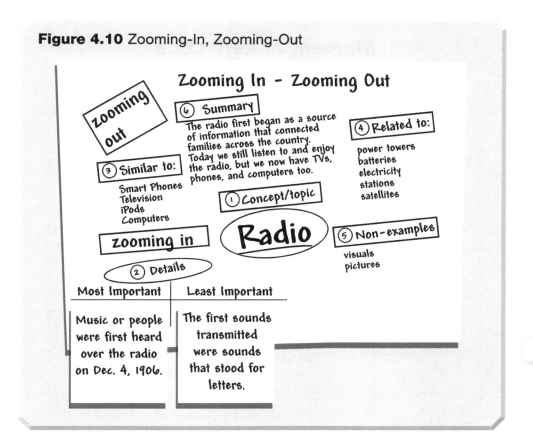

Differentiation: As with the other Comprehensible Input strategies, Zooming-In, Zooming-Out scaffolds the text for students by guiding them to move from details to big ideas one step at a time. The idea is to help students see *how* critical thinking looks. Critical thinking is a complex process that takes us into the text and beyond as we make sense of and process the information based on our own background knowledge and experiences.

Supporting English learners with content instruction requires teachers to continue to find ways to make explicit connections for them to new content and knowledge, as well as support students as they access the content. Teachers should continue to use a range of strategies to make content comprehensible and build bridges for learning. When students can connect with what they are learning, they can begin to see the relevance of learning and engage in successful learning experiences.

Moment of Reflection

1. What are the skills your students bring with them to the classroom? How have you been able to make connections for students between those skills brought from outside the classroom to those learned in school?

2. In what ways have you tried to make the content you are teaching comprehensible for students?

3. Think about all the great strategies you already use to support students in learning content while developing language. How can you share those strategies with your colleagues to ensure ELs are provided comprehensible input throughout the curriculum?

4. Think about the most difficult concepts or content you have taught your students in the past. How can you make that content come to life? What can you do to make it comprehensible for your students?

Chapter 5

Comprehensible Output

Anticipation Guide

Decide whether you agree or disagree with the statements below.

- As long as students are provided comprehensible input, they do not need comprehensible output.

- Pair-shares alone will help students build academic language and oral fluency.

- Students should speak with diverse partners to build strong academic language skills.

Let Students Use Language

With the shift toward integrated language and literacy approaches to learning, teachers and students have come to understand that comprehensible output is equally as important as comprehensible input. Students need to *use* language and literacy to access the content they are learning and also to share what they have learned. Comprehensible output gives students an opportunity to produce language (share knowledge) and develop fluency in expressing their thinking through authentic, frequent interactions. Students must be able to express their learning orally or through written forms as evidence of learning. Comprehensible input helps us learn language when the content and messages are understood; comprehensible output helps us express those ideas to communicate our thoughts and ideas with others.

We need to provide English learners multiple and varied opportunities to demonstrate learning. They have the ideas, and content is scaffolded in ways to maximize comprehension, so let's support them in sharing those ideas through language. It is through comprehensible output that teachers can further guide language development. Interactionist theories (Long and Porter 1985) emphasize this point as they look at the intersection of input and output. You cannot truly develop a second language at a level of academic fluency if you cannot access the information, understand it, interpret it, and in turn be able to express what you have learned. It is the output that provides a lens into the minds of students. We do not know what they have learned or what they understand if they don't show us (orally or in written forms). As students express learning, we can listen, look, and support as needed. It is through output that we can continue to explicitly guide learning and language. Without these opportunities, we limit students' language development opportunities.

Merrill Swain (1985) began research in the area of comprehensible output around the same time Stephen Krashen and Tracy Terrell shared their work on comprehensible input. However, at the time, the focus was primarily on understanding, or the input. What integrated approaches have revealed is that to understand, we must also be able to produce language. To be able to express through written or oral forms what we have learned helps us understand the information. And if students are to develop language, they have to use it. In my own experiences in some foreign language classes, we read and listened a lot. We listened to spoken dialogues, we read sentences to conjugate, but we didn't use the language orally or through authentic written forms, so we were never truly able to develop fluency. We can spend a great deal of time listening to and learning the language, but unless we use it, we don't fully develop it.

To become fluent in a language, we need to be able to communicate our thinking and our ideas about a range of content and topics. Integrated ELD can provide rich opportunities for comprehensible output. Across all disciplines, students are taught so much content and are exposed to a great deal of language related to that content, which provides a rigorous and authentic base from which to develop language. Students need to talk about what they are learning, write about it, and draw, design, and construct their learning to help develop academic language. Without sufficient opportunities to talk about content across the curricular areas, students will not develop the fluidity of expressing their thinking and learning for academic success.

To develop academic language, students need sufficient opportunities to express their learning. Deep Processing Theory (Craik and Lockhart 1972) reminds us of the need to interact with language multiple times and through varied exposures. To develop academic language, we need to be exposed to language, interact with language, revisit language, and use language. For example, if we want students to learn to express their understanding of how to multiply fractions, we need to show them how to do it, think aloud to model the language required to explain the process, have students try it out, revisit it again to address any misconceptions while still modeling language to explain the process, invite students to try it out again, have them share their processes with partners, revisit the processes, reflect, and then write about their thinking. These multiple exposures to the language and opportunities to use the language connected to the content being learned lead to *deep processing*. To learn something new, we need time with it; language is no different.

Comprehensible output provides students with opportunities to go deep in their learning and build fluency in academic language. What we need to keep in mind is the need to scaffold and guide output opportunities just as we do comprehensible input. Comprehensible output can be enhanced through questioning practices that facilitate rich discussions to structured opportunities to use language (strategies). Comprehensible output coupled with comprehensible input provides English learners with a full range of support for developing academic language.

Facilitating Discussions

An important and frequent approach to providing output opportunities is through discussions. Classroom discussions used daily in all disciplines provide students with a necessary range of language opportunities. Students get to practice explaining their thinking using a variety of academic and discipline-specific vocabulary, as well as practice using language for different language functions and forms. These are opportunities to talk and interact with peers using academic language. Discussions, when facilitated properly, lend themselves to developing a high level of academic language because they provide a platform for critical and creative oral discourse. The key is the proper facilitation of a discussion. There is no one way to do this, but there are definitely non-negotiables that define a discussion. Discussions must allow for an exchange of ideas, an opportunity to listen, challenge, extend, or defend ideas, and be able to draw from a range of perspectives. What I have noticed in my work with teachers is that we often say we engage students in daily discussions when we talk about texts or content, but I challenge you to think about two things: who was engaged in the discussion, and how were ideas being exchanged? Was it truly a discussion?

According to Google Dictionary, discussion can be defined as "the action or process of talking about something, typically to reach a decision or to exchange ideas; a conversation or debate about a certain topic." Key terms in this definition include *talking*, *exchanging ideas*, *debating*, and *reaching a decision*. When we engage students in discussions, they need to be presented with opportunities to not only share their ideas and hear other students' ideas, but to have those ideas discussed, dissected, argued, challenged, and/or extended by other students. Too often in our classrooms, we engage students in what we call "discussions" when in the end, only a few students share their ideas and we don't spend time debating those ideas. For example, after reading a chapter from *Island of the Blue Dolphins*, the teacher asked the class what trait they would associate with Karana, the protagonist of the story, and provide evidence to support their ideas. Students began sharing their ideas: "She was brave because she fought the wolves." Another student shared, "Karana was determined because she looked for materials at night to build her house and weapons." A final student shared, "I think she was helpful because she took care of the otter." This is what we would call a *grand conversation*; students take time to share their ideas and prove their thinking with evidence. A few students shared and then the teacher asked the next question. A discussion would warrant a much different process. Let's take the same question and student responses and see how it can be turned into a discussion.

> **Teacher:** *Now that we finished reading* Island of the Blue Dolphins, *what character traits do you think best represent Karana, and what evidence from the text supports your ideas?*
>
> **Sara:** *I think Karana is brave because she fought the wolves.*
>
> **Teacher:** *Can you share a little more about that? Why do you think fighting off wolves is brave? How does that show us she is brave?*
>
> **Sara:** *The wolves were wild, so even though she knows she could get hurt, she still risks her life. I think that is brave.*

Teacher: *Let's think about that idea and the trait of being brave. Does anyone else think that Karana is brave? Jonathan, you also thought she was brave, so you agree with Sara. What made you think Karana is brave? Did you have the same reason as Sara?*

The teacher spends time with Sara's idea before moving on. After Jonathan answers the follow-up question, the teacher could go on to ask, "Who agrees that Karana is brave? Turn and talk to your partner and explain whether you agree or disagree. Use evidence from the text to support your ideas." The teacher could call on a few more students to explain their perspectives on Karana being brave. As students share ideas, the teacher can make connections across ideas. During a discussion, if two students' ideas connect, it's important to emphasize that: "Aha, so your ideas were similar to _____. I see how the two of you drew from the same examples in the text." Another approach is to ask students to make those connections: "Did anyone hear ideas that were similar in what was shared? What did you hear?" Or, discuss the opposite: "Which perspectives differed?" After a few minutes, students can consider all the perspectives they heard and return to their partners to draw final conclusions about whether they think Karana is brave and why they think so now. This shows the differences between students just sharing out their ideas and listening, extending, arguing, and collaborating on ideas. They consider all the different ideas and perspectives to draw their own final conclusions. The discussion can then move on to another point of view: "Who came up with a different trait that describes Karana?"

From constructive conversations to precision partnering and talk moves, teachers use many different discussion formats and structured practices in the classroom. They all have the same end goal to engage students in an *exchange* of ideas, not just sharing ideas. Figure 5.1 (page 110) reminds us of the non-negotiables of a discussion. I encourage teachers to use all the great practices they have already learned for engaging students in discussions, but still reflect on those practices to determine if talk was maximized by all students and whether there was comprehensible output, or interaction and debate around thinking through language.

Figure 5.1 Defining Discussions

- Multiple perspectives shared
- Exchange of ideas
- Interact around ideas
- Debate and consider alternative perspectives
- Draw final conclusions (individual and collective)
- Listen, extend, or challenge ideas
- Defend ideas with evidence

Other considerations when facilitating a discussion include selecting the right material for a discussion, asking the right questions, and providing language supports as needed.

Selecting Texts

In order for discussions to take place, students need rich content to talk about. As content-area teachers, we are usually provided the content we are expected to teach through standards and curricula. To facilitate a discussion, we need to ensure that the content we teach is presented in a way that helps students consider the content through different perspectives. We want to use texts that challenge their thinking about the content and provide multiple perspectives or examples. In science, after reading a descriptive textbook chapter, we might use a supplemental article that presents a point of view illustrating the topic in the real world. For example, after reading a chapter on climate change, you might use a student-friendly article that shows different perspectives on climate change, with opinions from those who believe it is a scientific phenomenon and those who don't. These perspectives can be discussed alongside the factual textbook chapter for students to engage in a discussion.

The key to all discussions is proving your ideas! We want students to ground their conclusions in evidence. In mathematics, after teaching a particular process for solving a math problem from the book, present an alternative process, and students can discuss which they feel is most efficient or which they preferred for solving the problem. For example, when learning how to solve double-digit multiplication problems, students can be shown how to separate the two values by tens and ones to multiply, or teachers can show them the standard algorithm. Students can discuss why one method may be better or more efficient than the other or why learning multiple methods is important. English language arts, science, and social studies teachers might find some great resources online to juxtapose with textbooks for a rich discussion. Some of my favorites are **newsela.com** and Smithsonian's **tweentribune.com**. These sites have an abundance of great current events articles written for students at different grade levels and different reading levels. An important factor in selecting a text for discussion is ensuring that it is interesting. Find resources that make the topics students are learning about authentic and relevant to their lives. Where in the real world do they see the topics discussed or see common themes being presented and challenged? Selecting the right texts can be the first step toward a great discussion.

Generating Questions

Another key component to a great discussion is asking the right questions. Many tools are available to help teachers ask a range of questions. When I first started my teaching career, we used question stems from Bloom's Taxonomy; today, many teachers use tools for questioning at different Depth of Knowledge (DoK) levels. All these tools are helpful and can provide students with opportunities to think at a range of complex levels and use language for a variety of purposes. To facilitate a discussion, however, you want to make sure to ask the right questions.

I like to think about questions as factual, analytic, or evaluative. To not oversimplify how complex thinking can be, I will further connect Bloom's and DoK to the different levels to underscore the types of questions that can lead to great discussions. Factual questions are just that—questions that ask students to identify the facts, or the details that are revealed in the text. These are typically the traditional *who, what, when, where, how,* and *why* questions of a text. The answers to these questions are drawn directly from the text; we just need to find the answers and share what we found by extracting the details and facts. I like to think of these as questions that can be answered directly from the text, unlike analytic questions, where the answers are found in our heads. In content-area instruction, we have a tendency to focus on the factual questions. It makes sense because students are learning a plethora of new content, so we want to make sure they learn the facts and details. We need students to be able to summarize the stages of the life cycle of the butterfly, to explain the steps in solving an algebraic equation, and to know the different kings involved in the development of Mesopotamia. We are grounded in facts in content-area instruction. So we can start there, but we have to push further.

We want students to discuss their ideas and their perspectives about the content they are learning. "What would happen if the life cycle were interrupted?" "What are the most important steps in the cycle?" "Are there different ways to solve the equation?" "Were the leadership styles of kings ethical and/or equitable?" We want to challenge students to take the details, take the facts, and do something with that information—think about it further. When we ask students to act on content and knowledge, we push them from what is considered DoK level 1 (recall and reproduction) to DoK level 2 (skills and concepts), and then hopefully to DoK level 3 (strategic thinking). We do this by taking their thinking and pushing it toward a discussion, which takes us to analytic and evaluative questioning.

Analytic questions require students to analyze the facts and details. Thinking about the information in a way that goes beyond the text creates opportunities for analytic thinking. Factual answers are found in a text, but analyses are not—they have to come from within the student. I often tell students that they can't find these answers in the text because they are in their heads. They have to take the information learned and process it in some way. DoK level 2 helps us see some ways to act on the information. You can utilize a range of comprehension skills, such as compare and contrast, cause-and-effect relationships, etc., or conceptualize the information, such as determine author's purpose and find a main idea or theme. The act of using the information in some way, finding relationships, and connecting it to broader concepts or ideas is more complex, which is why it moves students into DoK level 2. But let's keep pushing, because it is not until we reach DoK level 3 and evaluative questions that we truly engage students in discussions.

Evaluative questions ask students to go beyond inferences and consider different perspectives and points of view. Students place value on the information, the ideas, the behaviors of characters, effectiveness of processes, and importance of decisions. Evaluative questioning further pulls in students' worlds. When we judge or place value on something, it is based on our experiences. Evaluative questions help students connect their learning to the outside world. It makes the learning relevant. For example, after reading *There Was an Old Lady Who Swallowed a Fly*, you might ask students if they think it was right for her to swallow a fly in the first place. Why or why not? Have you ever swallowed something you shouldn't have? These questions require that students place judgment or a value on something and relate it to their own experiences. Drawing out different perspectives and points of view can lead to rich discussions.

Analytic and evaluative questions connect with DoK level 3, strategic thinking. Students listen to different ideas, consider alternatives, debate, challenge, and draw on a range of experiences, evidence, and knowledge to prove their ideas. These are the types of questions and tasks that can best lead to rich discussions. To push the thinking even further, you can utilize a range of sources for students to consider as evidence or present different texts that share divergent perspectives, which allows you to push it to DoK level 4— extended thinking. At this level of complex thought, students consider more information from which to draw conclusions. Research projects are great for DoK level 4 because students have to use a variety of materials and are exposed to knowledge from multiple sources and need to synthesize them into logical arguments to defend. Overall, discussions cannot happen without the intentional planning and support of the teacher. We need to select the right materials, ask the right questions, and scaffold the language needed to engage in discussions. Figure 5.2 (pages 113–114) provides language supports teachers can provide for students to help them articulate their ideas.

Figure 5.2 Language Supports

"I think that...
I agree with [you] because I also think that...
I disagree with [you] because I don't think that..."

"I'm still confused...
Can you give me an example?
What about..."

"What do you mean by..?
Why do you think..?
I don't think...because..."

Figure 5.2 Language Supports *(cont.)*

Oral Rehearsals and Oral Language Practices (Strategies)

Discussions should remain an ongoing, daily practice in the classroom. They provide opportunities for English learners to rehearse and develop oral language skills. Coupled with discussions, teachers should also engage students in strategies that get students interacting with diverse partners. Students need to talk and share their ideas with students beyond those sitting at their tables. Pair-shares and table talks are great, but we also need students to hear and learn from different peers. This process allows for exposure to new perspectives and language models. The strategies presented for oral comprehensible output provide ideas for students engaging in oral language exchanges in different ways. Some strategies get students up and moving to talk with diverse partners, while other strategies ask them to be good listeners and engage in purposeful speech. These are just a few of the many wonderful strategies that truly engage students. Many teachers use strategies from Project GLAD® for oral language development, and they are very interactive. I encourage you to continue to use any strategies that have worked for you in your class. Ultimately, what is important is that students get opportunities to use academic English.

10-2

Purpose: A 10-2 lecture, much like a Stop-and-Jot, affords students opportunities to periodically reflect on their learning. The difference is that a 10-2 is an oral check-in, and a Stop-and-Jot provides more time for students to write notes or ideas they are learning about. A presentation of content that lasts for more than 10 minutes is a great deal of information for students to process. Based on brain research (Goldberg and Costa 1981), it is easier for students to process and remember information in smaller chunks. Students need to be able to stop to process what they are learning to help them remember the content.

Process: During a lesson, there are multiple times when teachers or students present content. Content can be presented through a lecture, reading, video, slide show, or any form of instruction where students are being given information. During the presentation of information, pause after about 10 minutes, and ask students to pause and think about what they have been learning. During this two-minute processing time, have students talk to partners and check in with their peers to see if they understand what is being taught. Continue this process periodically throughout the lesson after large chunks of information have been presented. It helps to stop and encourage students to think and talk at logical places in the text, such as at the end of a section header, short chapter, or after a few pages before the topic or story shifts. These stopping points help students track the information and remember what they are learning.

Differentiation: A 10-2 lecture presents a great opportunity for formative assessment. As students stop and think, walk around and answer any questions or clarify misinformation. If students are given an opportunity to talk with peers during the two minutes, listen in and help students as needed. This process further helps English learners to chunk the information so they are able to process the content being presented in English. Being able to check in with peers can further guide their learning.

3-Minute Share

Purpose: The purpose of a 3-minute share is for students to have an equitable opportunity to share what they have been learning. A 3-minute share is best used after students have completed reading or reviewing content and are ready to present what they learned to a small group. It can be used as a jigsaw where each member of the group is assigned to a given set of content to share during the 3-minute share.

Process: A 3-minute share will begin once students have learned content and are ready to share. Divide the class into groups of three or four students. Assign one member of the group as the timekeeper and another member of the group as the facilitator. Tell students that each member of the group is responsible for sharing the content they were assigned. For example, each member of the group may have had a different part of a long chapter to read, or each member might have read a different resource around a similar topic. Once everyone has read their assignment, have them share the information with their team. Each round of a 3-minute share goes as follows: The person sharing their content will have two minutes to present what was learned. During this time, the other members of the group must only listen; they cannot ask questions or contribute information. After the two minutes, the group now has one minute to ask questions or add to the information the speaker presented. For each part—the 2-minute share and the 1-minute questioning/clarifying—students must use the entire time. Even if students think they are done, encourage them to keep talking. Have each member of the group use the same process to share their information. A timekeeper is responsible for keeping track of the 2-minute share and 1-minute group question, and a facilitator will make sure everyone has a chance to share.

Differentiation: If there are newcomers or English learners at lower levels of ELD, pair them with classmates to read the same content and share together. When there is a partnership, the two minutes are shared between them; they are not each given two minutes. If ELs are not ready to verbalize, their partners can help, and it gives them a chance to participate when ready and listen to their peers as models of the English language.

Line-Up

Purpose: The purpose of a line-up is to provide students a chance to develop oral fluency while sharing their learning with multiple partners. A line-up is a strategy that can be used before, during, or after a lesson or unit of study. Students talk about their answers to a teacher's prompt or share what they have learned or produced.

Process: A line-up begins by providing students with something to talk about. You can give them a prompt to answer orally or in writing, or they can create some content. Once they have something to share or talk about, ask students to line up in two rows facing one another. You may need to create more than one line depending on the space in your classroom. Students will be standing up facing their partners. When directed, have students share their answers/content with the person standing in front of them, one at a time. After they have had a chance to share, call time and ask one line to move one partner over. One side should always stay stationary while the other line continues to rotate to the next person. Students should now have a new partner in front of them. Once again, have them share their answers/content with their new partners. Repeat this same process a few times so students can share with multiple partners.

Differentiation: A line-up is a great way to develop oral fluency because students have multiple opportunities to share what they learned. The repetition of the same information helps English learners orally rehearse and continue to improve how they are orally presenting their thinking after each repetition. Pair newcomers and students at lower levels of ELD with a classmate to move with along the line so that they can listen and learn from peer models of English. English learners who are able to express basic ideas or needs should be encouraged to participate independently, understanding that they are still learning. Also, encouraging them to practice articulating their ideas in English will help their language development.

Marble Talk

Purpose: The purpose of Marble Talk is for students to orally share their learning with multiple partners. Being able to interact with diverse partners is a great method for students to be exposed to different ideas and points of view as well as diverse language models. Marble Talk can be used to access prior knowledge by providing students an opportunity to talk about their background knowledge on a topic they will be studying, or after reading, viewing, or learning content.

Process: You will need a bag of marbles or any items that students will be able to grab in multiples (e.g., beans, pasta, buttons). Pass the bag around as students think about the topic or review their notes. Have students reach into the bag and pull out a handful of marbles (or whichever item you are using). Once everyone has a set, explain to students that they will be walking around the room and sharing what they know or have learned about the topic with their peers. What they don't know at this point is that the amount of information they have to share depends on the number of marbles they pulled from the bag. This is the fun part, as students who took a large amount realize they will have to share a great deal.

Ask students to find partners with a different number of marbles than they have, and then have each partner share the number of facts or ideas about the topic based on the number of marbles they have. For example, if a student pulled four marbles, they need to verbally share four facts they learned about the topic. Then, their partner will do the same for their number of marbles. After they finish, have students move on to talk with other partners. Walk around and help students find partners, and make sure students are moving along after sharing with their partners. Continue the activity for about five to seven minutes before having students return to their seats and collecting the marbles.

Differentiation: During Marble Talk, students will get multiple opportunities to share learning. English learners benefit from repeating their ideas in English as a form of oral fluency practice. It also helps ELs to interact with different partners to expose them to different ideas and models of English. As students walk around and share their ideas, it provides an opportunity to walk around and listen to what students are sharing, which is great formative assessment. Make sure to clarify any misinformation heard as students share with one another. A way to differentiate for students who need more practice using language is to have them use fewer marbles so they can share the same ideas multiple times.

Mix-Match-Dish

Purpose: Mix-Match-Dish is another great opportunity for students to develop oral fluency in English. During this activity, students will move around and interact with multiple partners to share what they have learned. A Mix-Match-Dish can be used prior to starting a unit of study as a method of accessing prior knowledge. It can also be used during or after a lesson once students have learned some content to talk about.

Process: Think about a topic, prompt, or content developed by students that they can talk about or share with their peers. Once students have something to talk about, ask them to stand up and push their chairs in because they will need space to move around the room. Have students walk around the room in no particular order or pattern—just slowly walk about the classroom. This walking is the *mixing* part. Make sure that they move around near one another. After a short amount of time, ask students to stop and call out a way for them to *match* up. This can be with a directive such as "find someone wearing the same color as you." Have students look around and find partners; assist them as necessary. Once they find partners, it's time to *dish*. Have students talk with one another about the topic or share the content they created. After about one to two minutes, call out, "Mix." Once again, ask students to start walking around. After a short period of time, call out, "Match up with someone who (provide a new matching criteria)." Have students look for new partners matching the criteria and *dish* by sharing what they learned or created. Repeat this process for a few rounds. Students enjoy the anticipation of hearing what the matching criteria will be.

Differentiation: As with many of the oral language strategies presented, Mix-Match-Dish is a great way for English learners to have repeated practice sharing their ideas in English. Repetition helps build their oral fluency while also interacting with multiple partners who contribute diverse ideas and English models. As students share with one another, it further provides a chance to listen in and hear what students know or have learned, which is yet another valuable formative assessment opportunity.

Written Output

Comprehensible output can be so engaging for students when we present a variety of activities for sharing learning. Whether we engage students in discussions or provide opportunities to write their ideas, the key is providing *frequent* and *ongoing* opportunities. The following strategies are just a few favorites that I have used in my own classroom for written output and continue to share with teachers working with English learners to support the development of written English fluency.

Cognitive Splash

Purpose: A great brainstorming strategy, Cognitive Splash engages all students simultaneously in recording ideas on paper. This strategy can be used as a preview activity to generate background knowledge, or it can be used after reading to see what students have learned. The purpose is to encourage students to just think and write freely while learning from others.

Process: Organize students into groups of three to five around a table. Place a large sheet of chart paper on the table. Fold the paper into fourths. In the center of the paper, write four topics you want students to brainstorm. Explain to students that they will all be writing simultaneously on the chart paper in the square closest to them. They don't have to write in the same direction (which could be challenging depending on the way they are seated); they should simply write on the chart in a way that is most comfortable for them. Start the activity, and have all students write at the same time in the square in front of them based on the topic at the top of their square. After about one to two minutes, ask students to finish their last ideas and rotate the chart paper clockwise so the next square is in front of them. Tell students to read what their classmates wrote and keep adding to the squares. Repeat this rotation process until the chart has been rotated three times, allowing everyone a chance to write in each square. An example is shown in Figure 5.3 (page 121). If there are only three students in a group, the activity should still follow the same process and the chart should rotate three times. If there is a group of five, two students can sit close enough together to reach the same square. (They should not work together, but just share the space.) You can use Cognitive Splash to see what students know about a topic before starting a unit or lesson, or use it after the lesson or unit of study to see what they have learned. One creative use for English learners is to write different phonics patterns in the center of the paper, with one in each square, so students can write as many words as they can think of with those patterns.

Differentiation: This strategy does require students to write, but it does not require them to write conventionally; it focuses on students getting their ideas on paper. We always want students to write properly, but if students are still developing their written English, this strategy does not require complete sentences and ideas. Students can also write words, phrases, details, or notes that capture what they know about the topics in the center of the chart. For above-level English learners, I recommend having students revisit every square at the end of the rotations, so they can discuss the most important details and any clarifications. I have pushed students to write a final definition for each of the topics written in the middle so they can synthesize all the information that was brainstormed. Each table can be assigned one of the topics to write the final definition and share it with the class.

Figure 5.3 Example of a Cognitive Splash

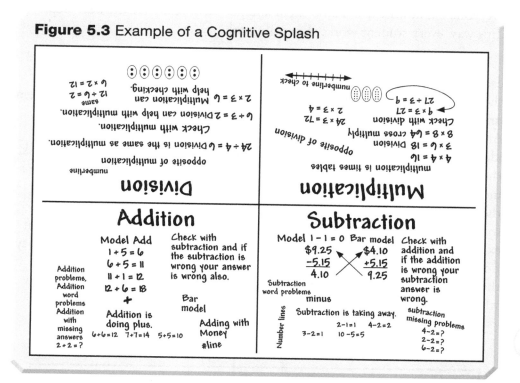

Give-One, Get-One

Purpose: Give-One, Get-One is one of the most versatile strategies and a favorite of students and teachers. This strategy is useful for generating background knowledge or can be used after students have learned content to assess comprehension. In Give-One, Get-One, students share with their classmates what they know or have learned and get ideas from their classmates in return.

Process: Begin by asking each student to fold a sheet of paper in half or to draw a line down the middle of their papers. Label one side *Give-One* and the other side *Get-One*. Provide students with a prompt or topic. Some examples include: five facts about the American Revolution, ten key details you learned about ecosystems, ten examples of figurative language, top five outcomes associated with the civil rights movement, or five different ways to make the number 25. Once students are given the prompt, ask them to write their lists on the *Give-One* side of the paper. I like to ask students for more information than I give them time for. For example, I'll ask for ten facts, but once I see everyone has at least five, I stop them and get them ready for the next step. This way, every student works the entire time.

Once students have their lists ready, explain that they will walk around and each give one idea from their lists to a peer, and in return, their peer will give them one idea back. When they get ideas from their peers, they will write them under the *Get-One* side. Students should only get one idea from each peer. After they get ideas and write them on the *Get-One* side and give their peers ideas, have them move on to other classmates to gather more ideas. I often ask them to reach for a target number, such as 10 new ideas. Again, I ask them for more ideas than I give them time for so that everyone is working and talking the entire time. I also challenge students by asking them to gather new ideas, so they cannot duplicate something that is already on their *Give-One* side. An example is shown in Figure 5.4. Ask students to return to their seats when they finish their last idea exchange. At this point, have the class share out some of the ideas that they wrote and gathered. Sharing encourages students to review what they have learned.

Figure 5.4 Student example of a Give-One, Get-One

The Coast

Give one

- Indians Build their homes in the coast
- There is a lot of water in the coast
- If you litter you might hurt the animals in the sea
- There is a lot of undersea animals
- There are indians that live in the coast

Get one

- Panama Canal
- They built the rattle that was a cocoon
- In the coast there is a lot of water

Differentiation: To help English learners at earlier levels of ELD, partner students to develop their *Give-One* lists, and have them walk around as a team getting more ideas from classmates. Working in teams helps students engage with multiple peers to expose them to a range of ideas and language models. I also like to challenge advanced English learners to write summary statements about what they learned based on the lists they gathered. Give-One, Get-One is one of those strategies that has the potential to keep kids learning. At the end of the activity, you can ask students to turn their papers over to create a final list called "Want-One." This is an opportunity for students to write additional questions about the topic that they still want answered. What do they still want to learn even after reflecting on their own and getting ideas and information from their peers? An example is shown in Figure 5.5. This is a great way to encourage ongoing learning as they generate more questions to explore further in class or on their own.

Figure 5.5 Student example of a Want-One

Write-Arounds

Purpose: Write-Arounds are fun methods for students to build upon one another's ideas. They can be used with any writing prompt or writing task provided to students. The idea is for students to read and comprehend what their peers write and then add on to the written text. This strategy helps students develop writing fluency.

Process: Group students into teams of four to six. Have each student begin with their own sheet of paper. Provide a prompt or an image to launch the writing. (You can provide a separate image or prompt for different students at each table group, or everyone can use one image or prompt.) For example, if you have a group of four, you can provide four different prompts or images to start the activity. The Write-Arounds will all still be different depending on how the first student starts the written text. All at once, have students write their responses to the prompt or begin developing stories behind the provided image. After about two minutes, ask students to finish their last sentences and pass their papers to the next student in the group. If they are around a table, have them pass their papers clockwise, and if they are in rows, have them pass their papers up or back to the next student. Once students receive new papers, have them read what their peers wrote and add on to the story/response. After about three to four minutes, ask students to finish their last sentences and once again pass their papers. Continue this process, asking students to read and add, until the papers get back to the original authors. An example is shown in Figure 5.6 (page 125). At this point, have each student share with their group the final stories/responses. Then, have students read their stories/responses out loud to their groups. (Students love this part! They really enjoy seeing the unique stories they create.)

Differentiation: Write-Arounds can also be done electronically through collaborative writing tools such as Google Docs, where students can write on shared documents. Have them use the same process as they take turns reading and adding to what the peers before them wrote. If there are students who are still developing at early stages of writing, pair them with classmates to brainstorm and write a response together. To challenge students after the activity, ask them to take their original papers back and write a final conclusion to the story/response.

Figure 5.6 Example of a Write-Around

There was a cat named Cathrine. Cathrine ^(lives in California) LOVES adventures. She has been to Hawaii, Florida, and Mexico. One morning, Cathrine was reading a newspaper and saw a coupon for a trip to Maine. "HURRAY!!! MAINE, HERE I COME!!!" Cathrine packed her bags to get ready for her trip the next day. "I can't wait until tommorow!" She says excidingly.

(9:00 PM, Friday Night)
"I should go to sleep. I have a busy day tommorow." Cathrine falls to sleep, dreaming of her big trip to Augusta, Maine. It was the next day (7:00am, Saturday morning). She said, happily, "It's finally the day im going to Augusta, Maine!" Cathrine grabbed her bags and ran out the door. She arrived at the airport and yelled "I'm going to Augusta Maine!" Cathrine was very exited but very tired when she got on the plane she fell fast asleep and slept for hours. When she woke up she noticed that the plane had stopped.

"This is your captain speaking. We have a problem with the plane. Just stay calm," the captain announced.

"Oh No!" Catherine says after hearing the announcement. She then sees people starting to panic and move around trying to figure out whats wrong. Catherine gets up out of her seat and tells everyone it's going to be ok. "I am a pilot."

Catherine runs to the front and tells the pilot he can land the plane. And everyone cheered and Catherine had fun in main.

Stop-and-Jot

Purpose: A Stop-and-Jot gives students time to reflect on their learning. It also continues to provide students with opportunities to develop their written fluency by frequently recording their learning in written form. The purpose of the Stop-and-Jot is to give students time periodically during lessons to write key ideas or details in their notes.

Process: This strategy can be used as part of any presentation of content, such as a lecture, a video, a slide show, a shared reading, a read-aloud, etc. Prepare for places during the presentation of the content to pause and provide students time to reflect on the content. When you pause, tell students, "Stop and think about what you have read/heard so far. What do you want to remember? What strikes you? Take a few seconds to think." Pause for a moment, then continue: "Now, write any key ideas or learning you don't want to forget." Provide students a minute or two to write some notes, and then continue to read or present information. Stop periodically to give students a chance to record their learning.

Differentiation: A Stop-and-Jot provides English learners think time to process the content being presented in English. It is also an opportunity to address any misunderstandings by walking around as students think and write before moving on in the lesson. Students at early levels of English language development can further check in with peers to see if they are missing any notes or ideas. Stop-and-Jots allow think time for English learners as they are working hard to process rich, new content and English at the same time.

List-Group-Label

Purpose: List-Group-Label is a preview or review strategy for students to share what they know or have learned. This activity goes beyond a brainstorm because it provides students time to work together to organize their ideas, which aids comprehension. As part of the lesson, students individually brainstorm their ideas, which gives them time to think first on their own, and then they share with others to deepen their understanding of the content.

Process: Provide students with small sticky notes and one sheet of chart paper for their table. Before studying content or after a unit of study, ask students to brainstorm for two or three minutes what they know or learned about the content. Individually, students should write one idea, detail, or key learning concept per sticky note. Be sure to remind them to use one sticky note per idea because they will be organizing them as part of the strategy. When students finish their individual brainstorming, ask them to combine all their sticky notes with students at their table. As a group, have them sort the sticky notes by categorizing and classifying their ideas. They can group the sticky notes in any way that makes sense to them. Then, have them organize their sticky notes on the chart paper and once they are nicely organized, have them add labels to the groupings to explain how they categorized the ideas. When all charts are complete, have students post them around the room for classmates to see. Review the different ways groups organized their ideas and if necessary, clarify any misconceptions or misinformation.

Differentiation: If necessary, pair English learners at lower levels with peers to create their initial brainstorms using the sticky notes. The group works together and collaboratively makes meaning from all their ideas. To challenge English learners at more advanced levels of ELD, mix up table group members, which requires members to share their charts with other group members. This is a great method for students to practice verbalizing their complex thinking.

Figure 5.7 Example of a List-Group-Label

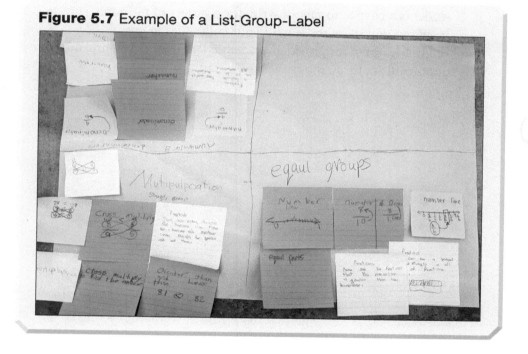

Comprehensible output cannot be forgotten if we are to provide students with optimal opportunities for developing academic English. Fluency in thought comes from the use of language. We need to think about, process, and express what we have learned. Vygotsky says it best: "A word devoid of thought is a dead thing, and a thought unembodied in words remains a shadow." Comprehensible input and output must go hand-in-hand if students are to develop language.

Moment of Reflection

1. What does it mean to engage students in a discussion?

2. Think about a recent discussion you led in your class. Did all students get a chance to participate? How were you able to maximize student participation?

3. How often do students in your classroom engage with a variety of partners beyond those sitting next to them or at their tables?

4. Think about all the strategies and activities you use to give students a chance to talk or write for a variety of purposes. How can you share those with your colleagues to ensure English learners are provided academic language development opportunities throughout the day?

Part III:
Writing Across All Content Areas

Chapter 6

Written Discourse

Anticipation Guide

Decide whether you agree or disagree with the statements below.

- Students learn how to write in English class.

- Writing for academic purposes is specific to each discipline.

- Providing writing tools helps English learners develop academic written English.

Providing the "Write" Access

As a child, I loved math. I started my college career as a math major because it was such a passion of mine. For me, math was easy to understand, it was easy to process, and I was able to apply my learning very easily. Although I loved math as a student, as a teacher and a professional developer, I love teaching about writing. I often think that perhaps my love for teaching writing came about because it was an area that I struggled with in school, but I didn't know I was struggling. All throughout elementary school and high school, I got As in my English classes and on writing assignments. In a book I wrote about teaching writing, I honored my high school Advanced Placement history teacher because she was the first person who stopped me and said, "You need help with your writing." Up until that point, I got by, and I didn't know I wasn't a good writer. It was then that I realized I needed to be a student of writing. I spent a lot of time working on my writing and deconstructing written texts to learn how they are put together and to understand the language that is used to clearly convey ideas for different purposes. My struggles early on as a writer made me more intentional in teaching writing.

131

What helps English learners is the guidance teachers can provide across the curriculum when students are asked to write for a variety of purposes. For me, it was exactly that; my history teacher showed me how to write. With her guidance and the time she spent deconstructing a thesis statement with me, I finally developed my written English skills.

Writing is a strong predictor of academic success. As students progress in school, writing becomes one of the main vehicles for demonstrating learning. With essays, reports, journals, notes, etc., students are constantly writing throughout the day and across content areas. If you think about your own experiences as you progressed through school, you will likely remember writing becoming more and more the primary vehicle for expressing what you learned as you advanced in your education. Think about your time in college or graduate school. You were consistently asked to write papers for your professors to evaluate your learning. Unfortunately, writing instruction has not received the same level of attention as reading instruction in elementary schools. There is a big push to develop students' literacy skills, understandably so, but literacy development includes writing.

Writing surrounds students' early literacy experiences. Children see writing all around them in the world. From signs and billboards to street names, students gain exposure to written language. At home, they may take crayons, pencils, or sidewalk chalk and draw scribbles and pictures that to them represent something very meaningful. They understand the purpose of writing as a method of conveying meaning and transmitting knowledge. Students have to learn to access writing and produce it. Reading is the focus in English language arts classrooms as students learn to access written language. Students develop foundational skills such as phonemic awareness, phonics, morphology, and concepts about print as building blocks that will help them learn to access written texts. They put sounds and letters together to read words, and they use knowledge of words and the world to determine the meaning of the text.

What we lose sight of sometimes is that this important work in early reading involves writing. Research on writing for English learners often emphasizes summarizing texts with students as a way to strengthen writing across the curriculum (Troia 2014). Reading and writing go hand in hand. When students read texts, they are decoding written language, which means they are learning to become writers themselves. They learn how letters are written and how to form sounds when reading words, and in turn, they use that knowledge to write their own words and sentences. As students continue to be exposed to reading and use what they are learning to write their own stories and texts, we need to be sure to guide this process as purposefully as we guide the reading of texts. Writing instruction needs the same level of guidance and importance as reading instruction. We need to guide students on how to write across the curricular areas as much as we help them read their textbooks and other content-area materials. We spend a great deal of time with the input, so we need to encourage and scaffold the output as well.

This chapter presents a range of the writing types students are asked to complete in different content areas with suggestions for how we can support students to be successful as they write about content. The chapters on comprehensible input and output shared the importance of how to help students access content and talk about it. This chapter goes deeper into how to scaffold written output and make it more explicit for students. A key to scaffolding writing during content-area instruction is to stay true to your discipline. Integrated ELD does not require that content-area teachers all become English language arts teachers, but to become teachers of the language of their discipline. As discussed in Chapter 3, content-area teachers should be teachers of academic language, functions, forms, and vocabulary; this chapter extends that idea to explain that writing provides access to more complex writing forms that serve different purposes, or in other words, written discourse structures. It is important to reflect as content-area teams or on your own about the writing opportunities you provide for your students and think about how you might need to scaffold the written tasks. How will the writing be presented? Is there a model to look at? Are there criteria to follow? Are there language tools or supports to help students express their ideas?

What Works in Writing Instruction?

Writing is a challenge for children. The National Assessment of Educational Progress (NAEP) reports that only 28% of adolescents are able to write proficiently for their grade level, 2% of students demonstrated advanced writing abilities, and 70% of students were below proficiency levels in writing. Students struggle for a variety of reasons, including poor knowledge of genre, too much focus on mechanics to revise, poor reading skills, or lack of writing fluency, and many students develop poor self-esteem and therefore lack motivation. When students struggle in an area, they have a tendency to self-regulate as they get older. By middle school, students begin to define themselves and their abilities as they relate to school. We hear students say, "I am not good in math. I am a terrible writer. I hate writing; I'm not good at it. I don't like to read. Reading is hard." These personal beliefs can transfer to the efforts students make in school.

Students' beliefs in their abilities and skills can cause them to self-regulate to the point of disengagement: "I am not going to bother to try on this writing assignment because I am not a good writer." They feel that their efforts are wasted on something they already believe they will fail. Gary Troia (2014) found the lack of student writing development can be caused by limited opportunities to write, and therefore students lack writing fluency. This is part of what was discussed when we talked about the emphasis on reading without the strong connections back to writing. Children need to write just as much as we encourage them to read if they are to develop fluency. How do we get good at something? We practice! We often ask students to read daily in the classroom and read at home for at least 20 minutes a day. How often do we ask them to do the same for writing? If students develop reading fluency by reading often, how do they develop writing fluency if we are not asking them to write as often? As I think back to my time in the classroom, I realize that I did not ask my students to write enough. Students should write for pleasure and to just get their ideas out, not only for formal written assignments. If students lack writing fluency, it can impact their success in content-area instruction because as they continue to progress in school, they will need to write with efficiency and frequency to keep up with their learning across disciplines.

In addition, Troia (2014) noted that students and teachers often focus too much on editing, so students lose sight of their ideas and can get frustrated. Part of their struggles are often found in their reading skills as well. When students do not read often, they are not exposed to written language frequently enough. They need to read a wide range of texts to see how language is crafted for different purposes and audiences. Reading often gives them ongoing access to writing. We should be explicit with students about the structures of written texts to remind them that what they are reading and how it is written is what we expect of them in their writing. Vocabulary, syntax, discourse, word choice, and idea development all present ongoing writing exposure that students can learn from to emulate and use as writers themselves.

Setting students up for success—making them feel from the beginning that they can and will be successful in the task at hand—changes students' motivation. As content-area teachers, we can provide the proper guidance and tools to show students how to present their ideas so they feel successful and *are* successful. Helping students see what we expect of them as writers and deconstructing writing with them will help them build the knowledge of writing across disciplines, and it will also give them the fluency they need to be successful in high-school- and college-level writing.

There are many positive practices teachers can use to support English learners as writers across the curriculum. Many teachers use graphic organizers, checklists, planning tools, prewriting opportunities, and outlines that continue to offer students excellent guides for how to capture and form their ideas. The NAEP writing results further suggest the use of word processors to support low-achieving writers, as they found that students who scored well on writing exams were knowledgeable of writing tools using word processors. This chapter continues with a focus on how to provide explicit instruction in how language is crafted to write for given purposes and audiences. This too has been proven through my own work with thousands of teachers, my own teaching in the classroom, and research that further supports the need to teach students about written discourse and genre to improve writing.

Written Genres

Students need to develop a strong understanding of genre (Gee 1996). When we ask students to write fictional narratives or an argumentative essay, they should understand the elements that comprise each type of writing as well as the discourse structures that guide how we organize our ideas. Students benefit from seeing a range of examples of the types of writing they are expected to produce. For example, if students need to write an argumentative essay in history class, history teachers do not have the time to explicitly teach them how to write the essay. But they can show students an example of what the essay should look like, accompanied by a tool that outlines the structure of the essay to guide students as they write. Students gather the information from a certain text type, but we often ask them to present the information in a different format. For example, they might read a textbook chapter, watch a video, and read a primary source document to gain evidence to support their argumentative essays. They are not exposed to the exact discourse structure we ask them to produce, so we need to provide examples of what is expected of them as writers. We want to set students up for success! They have the ideas, and teachers need to help them successfully put those ideas on paper.

For the work on twenty-first century literacies and for those states using college and career readiness standards, there are three main types of writing that are identified for students to produce:

- to persuade, in order to change the reader's point of view or affect the reader's action (Opinion/Argumentative)

- to explain, in order to expand a reader's understanding (Informational/Explanatory)

- to convey experience (real or imagined), in order to communicate individual and imagined experiences to others (Narrative Accounts)

In my work with content-area teachers in integrated ELD, I emphasize the need to stay focused on the writing of your discipline. Think about the opportunities students have to write in their specific content areas that are opinion/argumentative, informational/explanatory, and narrative. Starting there helps us identify the writing tasks for which we may need to provide proper tools and language supports to guide the writing. Figure 6.1 (pages 137–139) shows a list of writing tasks that teachers from across the country have shared with me, and they expect students to complete the tasks as part of their content-area instruction.

Figure 6.1 Writing Across the Curriculum

	Narrative	Informational/ Explanatory	Opinion/ Argumentative
English Language Arts	Fictional narratives Personal narratives Science fiction narratives Historical fiction narratives Narrative poems Personal stories/ experiences Biographies Folk tales Memoirs Legends Daily journals Fictional stories Songs	Reports Informational essays Concrete summaries Brochures Time lines Literary nonfiction Multimedia presentations Recipes How-tos College applications Resumes	Argumentative essays Persuasive letter/essays Debates Opinion-Editorial (op/ed) pieces Literary analyses Abstract summaries Advertisements Commercials Web pages

Figure 6.1 Writing Across the Curriculum *(cont.)*

	Narrative	Informational/ Explanatory	Opinion/ Argumentative
Science	Simulated science journals	Science reports Informational essays Concrete summaries Science journals Biographies Comparative essays Informational presentations Diagrams Tables/Charts	Advertisements Critiques T-charts College entrance exams Persuasive essays Timed writings Exit slips Written dialogues
History/ Social Science	Simulated historical journal entries Simulated historical letters Historical diaries Fictional stories Poems Songs Postcards	Newspaper articles Reports Exit slips Bubble webs Venn diagrams Cause-and-effect tables Chronological time lines Scripts Summaries Research papers Compare and contrast essays Maps	

Figure 6.1 Writing Across the Curriculum *(cont.)*

	Narrative	**Informational/ Explanatory**	**Opinion/ Argumentative**
Mathematics	Word problems can be written as short narrative stories.	Procedural explanations Exit slips Diagrams Concrete procedural	Opinion-based procedural explanations

Once teachers have selected a written product for students to produce so they may demonstrate what they have learned or are learning, explicit tools can be provided to guide the writing. Written discourse frames with language stems are helpful tools for students to use when crafting their ideas. Integrated ELD doesn't expect all teachers to teach the writing process over a long period of time as an English teacher would, but to provide access to what the writing should look like and how students can form their ideas. I like to start by identifying the elements or the criteria expected for the written task. Figure 6.2 (page 140) is an example of a written task deconstructed to identify key elements the teacher expects for a personal narrative. This can be provided to students, or it can be created with students by deconstructing a sample together.

Figure 6.2 Deconstructed Writing Task

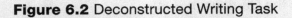

Personal Narrative

- Hook – title/opening
- Dialog(ue)
- Introduction – setting, introducing the characters.

• First person point of view

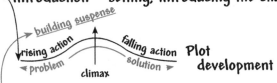

building suspense

rising action

falling action

problem

climax

solution

Plot development

- Figurative language
  - simile
  - personification
  - onomatopoeia
  - metaphors

- imagery – vivid verbs (synonyms) • foreshadowing

Once you know what the criteria or the elements of the written task will be, continue by identifying any potential language supports that can further help students put their ideas in writing. Figure 6.3 (page 141) is an example of how the tool for students to write a personal reflection was further developed to include language supports. These supports can include sentence frames, key vocabulary, or language cues (such as transition words) that students can use to form their ideas in writing. The language support column provides multiple ways of expressing language. Options are important because students are at different levels and need a range of supports. I like to call these tools *language discourse frames* because they provide the criteria or outline of written tasks, as well as the language to express their ideas. Tools such as these language discourse frames do not have to be taught explicitly over a long period of time during content-area instruction. They can if they are part of the objective, such as an ELA teacher teaching personal reflection or a science teacher teaching lab reports, but they should be provided to students as tools to guide them after they have learned from you and just need help getting those ideas on paper. A wide range of these language discourse frames across content areas are provided in the appendixes.

Figure 6.3 Language Discourse Frames

Personal Reflection	
Elements/Criteria	**Language Support**
Opening: Establish the context.	I remember…
• When it took place	I can remember…
• Where were you?	I remember when…
• Who was there?	When I was…
Narrate the event.	Last year…
—introduce characters, people	One time…
—sequence the event	Once…
Conclusion: Establish the memorable moment.	It started when…
• Why was it a memorable event?	Ordinal words (first, then, next, following, after)
• What did you learn?	Descriptive language
• How did you feel?	Dialogue
	Feelings/emotions
	I'll never forget…
	I will always remember…
	This was why…
	I learned…
	I realized…
	It changed me because…
	The great part about it was…
	That day I learned…

For integrated ELD to work, and for all content-area teachers to feel comfortable and capable of teaching language in their discipline, they need to feel that teaching writing is a natural part of their work in their content area. Writing is one of those tasks that can take a great deal of time to teach, revise, and edit and revise again; but content-area teachers do not have that time, unless it is their objective for the day. Anytime we ask students to write in the content areas, we need to remind ourselves that it requires academic language. English learners need support to craft their ideas so they may express everything they have learned. Providing tools such as language discourse frames or procedural prompts and organizers can be an effective method for all educators to be teachers of written academic language.

Make it work for you and your students so it feels like a natural part of your instruction. Provide students with tools and access to language that aligns with your expectations of them as writers in your discipline. Keep in mind that not all English learners will be able to produce the same level of written English. But you are providing the tools, so every time they write, they will continue to develop their writing fluency, and the sophistication of their writing will increase because you provided models. You showed them where to go next as writers. Be patient: beginning level English learners are learning, they are seeing how to write, they are taking everything in, and when they are ready, they will put more down on paper. For now, you are giving them the platform to do what they can and see where they are headed. Intermediate and advanced English language learners are not only given the criteria for strong academic writing, but also a range of possible language structures to help them form their ideas. These language discourse frames help the range of ELs in your class to continue progressing at their own levels.

Moment of Reflection

1. Do your students have multiple opportunities to write throughout the day?

2. Think about a recent writing assignment in your class. Did all students have the tools they needed to be successful with the assignment?

3. How can language discourse frames help to support your students' growth as writers?

4. Think about all the strategies and activities you use to help students become stronger writers. How can you share those with your colleagues to ensure English learners are provided sufficient writing support throughout the day?

Part IV: Concluding Thoughts

Completing the Puzzle

Learning a new language is difficult for all of us. This, coupled with learning a wide range of challenging content in the new language, makes the experience even more demanding. As teachers, we are tasked with helping students navigate these experiences. But this is not new information; we know and have known for years that teaching is hard work. We have experienced days in our classrooms where we feel helpless and frustrated because it doesn't seem like we are getting through to our students. But we have more days when we experience the pure joy of watching students connect the puzzle pieces of learning. This is the balance of teaching—learning from the challenges and creating successes from those experiences. I am inspired every time I enter a classroom because I get to see teachers and students working together to find this balance. It is truly a shared experience and I have had the privilege of being part of these experiences through the work I present from my research, my teaching, and my own struggles to find balance in the classroom. Sometimes we can feel alone in our work, but know that you are not alone—we all struggle. Teaching is a journey, and I am hopeful that this book will help you feel supported along the way.

Guiding students in learning language takes time. To gain a level of academic language proficiency in a language takes years. We don't always see the learning take place, but know that your intentional teaching and care for your students is contributing to daily, successful language- and content-learning experiences. In one of my graduate level courses, a student shared with me that she was feeling disappointed in her teaching because she didn't think she was reaching her English learners. We talked about her lessons and how she was intentionally developing integrated ELD lessons that called out language, scaffolded content, explicitly provided language cues, brought learning to life, and gave students opportunities to make mistakes and practice using language to share their learning. All of her planning was developed through a very specific lens of how to make language explicit and guide all students to learn content and develop academic language. I shared with this student that she was making a difference. We can't always see the impact of our teaching right away. Language development takes time. As long as we are being intentional and accountable for presenting strong integrated ELD lessons, we are providing those connecting puzzle pieces for students. Academic language development takes years to be able to demonstrate at a high cognitive and linguistic level. English learners will have pivotal turning points of learning along the way, but we must be patient with ourselves and our students in getting there. This is not to say we don't hold students to high expectations—we do! But we need to feel good about the work we do. If we are being intentional and thorough in how we plan for and support English learners, then we are serving them well. Trust that they will learn. I offered the reflective questions at the end of each chapter in an attempt to encourage a conversation, just as I do with my graduate students. Reflection can help us hold ourselves accountable for how we are supporting our English learners. I am hopeful that you will take time to reflect on your teaching and continue to use the reflective questions as a guide to keep your teaching intentional, rigorous, and impactful.

The ideas, practices, and strategies presented in this book are just some of the many wonderful instructional approaches that have been implemented to support English learners. Many of us have used these strategies for years and I am hopeful that reading this book reinforced the great work you are already doing. It can be refreshing and reassuring to read a book that validates our teaching and gives us some new ideas. For those of us who are new to this work, know that it is challenging, but committing to professional growth demonstrates dedication to your students. Over time, you will find yourself designing your own strategies and modifying the many that are already in the field. The more you learn about your students, the more you learn about language development. As you continue to learn about teaching and instruction, you will find what works best for you and your students. Your teaching will become organic, and every year, as you meet your new students, you will draw from a range of approaches that can guide your daily instruction. What continues to inspire me in my work around language education is knowing that teachers, novice and experienced alike, strive to connect content and language for students. Every meaningful lesson offers English learners one more piece to help them complete the puzzle of academic success.

Narrative Writing Language Supports

Biographical Brochure

Elements/Criteria	Language Supports
Biographical Events • Birth • Hometown • Formative years • Education/Jobs • Influences/Contributions • Famous quotes • Current status/Death	He/She was born… As a student he/she… He/She lived… As a child… He/She worked in… He/She attended… His/Her mentors were… His/Her works include… He/She was known as… He/She also wrote… He/She believed… He/She died… He/She currently…

Narrative Writing Language Supports *(cont.)*

Graphic Novels/Comics

Elements/Criteria	Language Supports
Introduction • Setting • Characters	Dialogue Characters Visuals Dynamic Figurative Language Static Onomatopoeia
Plot • Sequential • Conflict • R.A., F.A. • Climax • Resolution	**Vocabulary** • Conflict • Plot diagram • Elements of Fiction/Nonfiction • Character development
Extension Activities • One page analysis • Analyze number of frames	**Vocabulary specific to genre** • Show versus tell

Narrative Writing Language Supports *(cont.)*

Fairy Tale

Overall features: past tense/third person

Elements/Criteria	Language Supports
• Characters—good/evil • Setting • Magical—larger than life • Elements of three • Royalty	Once upon a time… In a far away land… Long, long ago… Cue words: magical…
Describe the event • Problem/conflict • Dialogue • Sequence	At first… Cue words: next, before, then, finally
Conclusion • Resolution • Lesson learned	They lived happily ever after… The End. Cue words: however, still, suppose

Narrative Writing Language Supports *(cont.)*

News Story

Elements/Criteria	Language Supports
Title Intro Event—set the scene • Backstory	• It all started when... • It all took place in/during/at a time when... • In response to...
Timeline of Events • Eyewitness account	• I saw/witnessed... • I experienced... • I felt... • First, next, then...
Outcome • Statistics • Number of dead • Community fears/concerns/emotions	• Afterwards... • This resulted in... • This created...
Lasting Impact	• Because of this... • As a result of... • This led to...

Informational Writing Language Supports

What Is Informational Writing?

Purpose: A nonfiction report aims to inform the reader about a topic using information, facts, and details.

Structure:	**Text Features:**
• A topic • Topic sentence • Facts • Summary	• Pictures • Diagrams • Headings • Labels • Captions • Bold print
Grammar:	**Forms:**
• Linking words and phrases • Present tense • Technical tense • Nouns • Adjectives	• Descriptions • Lists • Sequences • Compare and contrasts • Cause and effects

Informational Writing Language Supports *(cont.)*

Expository (Body) Paragraph

Elements/Criteria	Language Supports
Establish Topic • Who, what, where, when, why, how • Establish sequence. (first…? second…? last…?)	…was about… First I want to talk about… To begin with… Cues: first, second, last
Details Describing Topic • Facts about topic • Experience with topic • Citing textual evidence	Based on… Some people know that… According to… The text says… Cues: text, reason, evidence, because
Transition Statement • Summarize what the paragraph said about the topic.	This is why… Therefore… Cues: (topic word) therefore, finally

Informational Writing Language Supports *(cont.)*

Factual Writing for the Purpose of Informing Others

Elements/Criteria	Language
Introduction Paragraph • Thesis statement/controlling idea • Topic sentence • Central Idea • Attention grabber/hook	I am going to explain… I am going to persuade you to… The text was about… Based on the text… It is clear that… It is evident that…
Body Paragraphs • Main idea • Facts/supporting details • Golden brick (quotes, statistics…)	Cue words: for example, one reason, one way, etc. secondly, lastly, etc.
Conclusion • R A P • R–restate • A–advice • P–predict	Cue words: in conclusion, overall… My advice to you is that… I just explained…

Informational Writing Language Supports *(cont.)*

Informational Report (Animals)

Elements/Criteria	Language Supports
Title (Topic) Introduction • Lead • Questions (inquiry) • Quote (cool fact) • Questions (inquiry)	• Did you know... • According to... • ...are fascinating. Did you know they...
Description of the Topic • Physical description • Location/habitat • Diet	...are... ...have... ...like to... Their diet consists of... Their habitat is... They live in...
Purpose/Role/Importance	The role of...in... ...are important because... The purpose of... ...play a role in...
Interesting Facts (Fun Facts)	Did you know that...? Some interesting things about... Some fun facts about...are...
Personal Connection	I wish... I learned... Something that surprised me was... I found it interesting that...

Opinion/Argumentative Writing Language Supports

Argumentative Paragraph (Anchor Chart)

(Defend a claim)

Elements State the Claim	Language Supports
Evidence #1 • facts, data, statistics, quote, example Evidence #2 • facts, data, statistics, quote, example Evidence #3 • facts, data, statistics, quote, example Conclusion (restate your claim)	For example... You can see that... In addition... Therefore... This proves that... ...is... ...says... Another example...

Opinion/Argumentative Writing Language Supports *(cont.)*

Paragraph with Argument

Overall feature: 5–8 sentences

Elements/Criteria	Language Supports
Top sentence • main idea ⬇ • position	My position… I think… I believe… I'm against… because… I favor…
Supporting Details • data • details • facts • quotes • examples • statistics	According to research… Studies show… According to some facts… Based on… As a result of… …states…
Conclusion • restate main idea	Finally… Therefore…

Opinion/Argumentative Writing Language Supports *(cont.)*

Opinion Essay (Anchor Chart)

Elements/Criteria	Language Supports
Introduction • Hook • Thesis	I believe/in my opinion… I think… The main idea of… I would argue… The author states… The author believes…
Body Paragraphs • Support (quotes, facts, statistics, examples)	My first reason… One reason… For example… For instance… Although/however… Based on…
Conclusion • Restate your thesis • Bring the reader back to the main argument • Next steps/new ideas to consider • Leave the reader with something to keep thinking about	In conclusion… For this reason… In the end…

Opinion/Argumentative Writing Language Supports *(cont.)*

Opinion Essay

Elements/Criteria	Language Supports
Introduction • Connect to audience (make the topic relevant) • Thesis (Position)	Many argue… Others believe… My opinion is… Research shows…
Supporting Paragraph(s) • Introduce the main point (connected to thesis) • Evidence (reasons, examples, explanations, quotes, data) • Alternative point of view • Conclusion • Transition (to next paragraph)	The (text/article) says… Others agree… Based on… Others might think that… However… Evidence shows that…
Conclusion • Relevance (big idea)	In conclusion… The view of… In relation to… This is important because…

Opinion/Argumentative Writing Language Supports *(cont.)*

Stance Paper

Criteria/Discourse	Language Supports
First paragraph—Stance	I believe… I think… I feel… Based on, I would argue…
Supporting Paragraph(s) • Data • Facts • Examples • Details	For example… For instance… Data shows…
Third Paragraph—Pro Statement	…favor… An advantage… …would agree that…
Fourth Paragraph—Con Statement • Rebuttal	One drawback… A disadvantage might be… …disagrees because…
Fifth Paragraph—Conclusion	This is why… This proves that…

Math and Science Language Supports

Which Process Is Better?

Elements/Criteria	Language Supports
Set up and state your purpose	In order to solve system of equations… There are three ways to solve systems, I chose…because… I prefer to use… I'm learning…
Describe how to solve	First… Second… Then… Finally…
Explain why	I chose…because… …is the best method because… For this system…was best because…

Math and Science Language Supports *(cont.)*

Process Paragraph (Math)

Elements/Criteria	Language Supports
Identify the problem.	• Today, we need to find… • Problem # … stated… • The problem asked us to…
Explain the steps taken to solve the problem.	• I got my answer by… • To solve… I… • I needed to… • I started by… • First, next, then
Provide the final answer.	I chose…because… …is the best method because… For this system…was best because…
Extension • Alternative solution	• You can also solve this by… • Another way to solve the problem is…

Math and Science Language Supports *(cont.)*

Math/Science
Summary Conclusion

Elements/Criteria	Language Supports
Claim • Answer the original question • Based on the observation • Factual statement	…occurs because… The solution is… …is…because…
Evidence • Supports the claim • Description of evidence • Vocabulary • Refers to graphs, tables, etc.	The evidence shows… The graph shows… The lab proves… The data proves…
Reasoning • Specific content and academic vocabulary • Connects evidence to claim • Sufficient concept principals	This makes sense because… This proves that…

Math and Science Language Supports *(cont.)*

Lab Report

Criteria/Discourse	Language Supports
Abstract • Introduction • What you did and why • Background info • Hypothesis • Purpose	We sought to find out… The purpose of the lab was… If…then… This lab helps us learn about… In this lab, we will be testing… We tested…
Methods and Procedures • Equipment used • Process steps • Safety	The equipment we used was… First, Second, Third, Next, And then, Finally The safety procedures we followed were… (List equipment used)
Results/Conclusions • Data calculations and analysis • Observations • Graphs or tables • Analyze hypothesis • Tie back to the purpose	Our results showed… From our data, we conclude… I proved my hypothesis because… I disproved my hypothesis because… I/We found that… Our data supports/does not support… We observed…

Math and Science Language Supports *(cont.)*

Science Lab Analysis

Elements	Language Supports
Explain data in words. Did findings support hypothesis? Significance of errors Relate findings to the real world. Make inferences based on findings.	• The data shows… • From the graph… • The data trends are… • The data supports the hypothesis because… • The data does not support the hypothesis because… • An error that occured was… • …could have impacted the data by… • In future labs… • The significance of these findings… • Based on this data, we can conclude… • The data/lab supports the…law/theory. • From the data, we can infer… • There is a…correlation between… and…variable.

Summaries/Reports Language Supports

Relating Text to Self

Elements/Criteria	Language Supports
Establish Connection	I relate to…because…
Give example of connection	The similarities between…and…are… In…I have also…
How the connection leads to objective/perspective	For instance… When I was…she…; I… Another example is…
Leads to alternate resolution	I learned… Because…, … Like…, …

Summaries/Reports Language Supports *(cont.)*

Concrete Summary (Fiction)

Elements/Criteria	Language Supports
Establish the <u>exposition</u> or background.	The story begins with… In the beginning of the story… The story introduces…
Describe the key events.	So what happened was… First, second, next, eventually, before, during, after, finally, lastly
Wrap-Up • The "takeaway" • Lesson learned • Main idea • Theme • Purpose	The reader understands… The characters learned… The writer/author demonstrates…

Summaries/Reports Language Supports *(cont.)*

Concrete Summary (Nonfiction)

Elements/Criteria	Language Supports
Establish Connection • the what/event • time/people involved • the process • main idea	In…, …happens. …is when… This was mostly about… The main idea of the event… Research showed…
Expand on Main Points • details • facts • quote important phrases	For example… Then, after, finally… Research showed… According to… One impact was… This lead to…
Conclusion • overall summary • emphasize main idea	Overall… In summary… The most important thing to remember is…

Report (K–1st)

Cover Page
- Title
- Author/Illustrator
- Date
- Picture

Pictures with Caption
- Detail/Facts

Diagram
- Title
- Labeled diagram

Summaries/Reports Language Supports *(cont.)*

Report (1st–2nd)

Cover Page
- Title
- Author/Illustrator
- Date
- Picture/Illustration

Body of the Report
- Topic sentence
- Facts

Personal Connection

- What surprised you?
- What was your takeaway?
- What did you learn most?
- What are your next learning steps?

- I was surprised to learn...
- It was so interesting to learn that...
- I'll always remember...
- I am curious to learn more about...
- I now wonder...

Summaries/Reports Language Supports *(cont.)*

Report (3rd-5th)

Cover Page
- Title
- Author/Illustrator
- Date
- Picture/Diagram

Introductory Paragraph
- Invite the reader in (You)
- Quote, action, interesting fact, statistic
- Topic sentence
- Introduce subtopics (categories you will talk about)
- Concluding/transition sentence

Second Paragraph (Body Paragraph)
- Topic sentence
- 2–3 sentences of key facts, details, data about the topic
- An interesting fact
- Concluding/transition sentence

Third Paragraph (Body Paragraph)
- Topic sentence
- 2–3 sentences of key facts, details, examples data about the topic
- An interesting fact
- Concluding/transition sentence

Personal Connection
- What surprised you?
- What were you most impressed by?
- What are your next steps in your learning?
- What further questions do you have?
- Recommendation
- Final reflection (feels, what you liked or didn't like)

Digital Resources

Accessing the Digital Resources

1. Go to **www.tcmpub.com/digital**

2. Enter the ISBN, which is located on the back cover of the book, into the appropriate field on the website.

3. Respond to the prompts using the book to view your account and available digital content.

4. Choose the digital resources you would like to download. You can download all the files at once, or you can download a specific group of files.

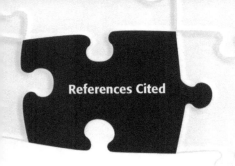

Anderson, Richard C. 1977. "The Notion of Schemata and the Educational Enterprise." In *Schooling and the Acquisition of Knowledge*, edited by Richard C. Anderson, Rand J. Spiro, and William E. Montague, 415–431. Hillsdale, NJ: Lawrence Erlbaum Associates.

———. 1994. "Role of Reader's Schema in Comprehension, Learning, and Memory." In *Theoretical Models and Processes of Reading*, 4th ed., edited by Robert B. Ruddell, Martha Rapp Ruddell, and Harry Singer, 469–482. Newark, DE: International Reading Association.

Anderson, Richard C., and William E. Nagy. 1992. "The Vocabulary Conundrum." *American Educator* 16, no. 4 (Winter): 14–18, 44–47.

Beck, Isabel L., Margaret G. McKeown, and Linda Kucan. 2002. *Bringing Words to Life: Robust Vocabulary Instruction*. New York: Guilford Press. 15–30.

Biemiller, Andrew. 2005. "Vocabulary Development and Instruction: A Prerequisite for School Learning." In *Handbook of Early Literacy Research (Vol 2)*, edited by Susan Neuman and David Dickinson, 41–51. New York: Guilford Press.

California Department of Education. 2014. "Chapter 2: Essential Considerations in ELA/Literacy and ELD Curriculum, Instruction, and Assessment." In *California English Language Arts/English Language Development Framework for California Public Schools*, edited by California Department of Education, 51–128. Sacramento: California Department of Education.

Collier, Virginia P. 1989. "How Long? A Synthesis of Research on Academic Achievement in a Second Language. *TESOL Quarterly* 23, no. 3 (September): 509–531.

Craik, Fergus I. M., and Robert S. Lockhart. 1972. "Levels of Processing: A Framework for Memory Research." *Journal of Verbal Learning and Verbal Behavior* 11: 671–684.

Cummins, Jim. 1981. "The Role of Primary Language Development in Promoting Educational Success for Language Minority Students." In *Schooling and Language Minority Students: A Theoretical Framework*, edited by California State Department of Education, 3–49. Los Angeles: National Dissemination and Assessment Center.

———. 1984. *Bilingualism and Special Education: Issues in Assessment and Pedagogy.* San Diego: College Hill.

———. 1991. "Language Development and Academic Learning." In *Language, Culture, and Cognition*, edited by Lilliam Malave and Georges Duquette, 161–175. Clevedon, UK: Multilingual Matters.

———. 1994. "The Acquisition of English as a Second Language." In *Kids Come in All Languages: Reading Instruction for ESL Students*, edited by Karen Spangenberg-Urbschat and Robert Pritchard, 36–62. Delaware: International Reading Association.

———. 2000. *Language, Power and Pedagogy: Bilingual Children in the Crossfire.* Clevedon, UK: Multilingual Matters.

———. 2003. "Reading and the Bilingual Student: Fact and Friction." In *English Learners: Reading the Highest Level of English Literacy*, edited by Gilbert G. Garcia, 2–33. Newark, DE: International Reading Association.

Cummins, Jim, and Sharon McNeely. 1987. "Language Development, Academic Learning, and Empowering Minority Students." In *Bilingual Education and Bilingual Special Education: A Guide for Administrators*, edited by Sandra H. Fradd and William J. Tikunoff, 75–94. Boston: College Hill.

Dutro, Susana. 2015. "Teaching ELD: What Every Educator Ought to Know." *E.L. Achieve* (blog). December 2, 2015. http://www.elachieve.org/blog/teaching-eld-what-every-educator-ought-to-know.html.

Dutro, Susana, and Carrol Moran. 2003. "Rethinking English Language Instruction: An Architectural Approach." In *English Learners: Reaching the Highest Level of English Literacy*, edited by Gilbert G. García, 227–258. Newark, DE: International Reading Association.

Dutro, Susana, and Kate Kinsella. 2010. "English Language Development: Issues and Implementation at Grades Six Through Twelve." In *Improving Education for English Learners: Research-Based Approaches*, edited by California Department of Education, 151–207. Sacramento: California Department of Education Press.

Echeverria, Jana, and Deborah Short. 2010. "Programs and Practices for Effective Sheltered Content Instruction." In *Improving Education for English Learners: Research-Based Approaches*, edited by California Department of Education, 251–321. Sacramento: California Department of Education Press.

Gee, James Paul. (1991) 1996. *Social Linguistics and Literacies: Ideology in Discourses*. London: Taylor & Francis.

Girard, Vanessa, and Pam Spycher. 2007. "Deconstructing Language for English Learners." *Aiming High* (March): 1–8. Santa Rosa, CA: Sonoma County Office of Education.

Goldberg, Elkhonon, and Louis D. Costa. 1981. "Hemisphere Differences in the Acquisition and Use of Descriptive Systems." *Brain and Language* 14, no. 1: 144–173.

Hollie, Sharroky. 2012. *Culturally and Linguistically Responsive Teaching and Learning*. Huntington Beach, CA: Shell Education.

Jenkins, Henry. 2009. *Confronting the Challenges of Participatory Culture: Media Education for the 21st Century*. Chicago: The MacArthur Foundation.

Krashen, Stephen D. 1985. *The Input Hypothesis: Issues and Implications*. Boston, MA: Addison-Wesley Longman Ltd.

Krashen, Stephen D., and Tracy D. Terrell. 1983. *The Natural Approach: Language Acquisition in the Classroom*. Hayward, CA: Alemany Press.

Long, Michael H., and Patricia A. Porter. 1985. "Group Work, Interlanguage Talk, and Second Language Acquisition." *TESOL Quarterly* 19, no. 2 (June): 207–228.

MacSwan, Jeff, and Kellie Rolstad. 2003. "Linguistic Diversity, Schooling, and Social Class: Rethinking Our Conception of Language Proficiency in Language Minority Education." In *Sociolinguistics: The Essential Reading*s, edited by Christina Bratt Paulston and G. Richard Tucker, 329–340. Oxford: Blackwell Publishing Ltd.

Marzano, Robert J. 2004. *Building Background Knowledge for Academic Achievement: Research on What Works in Schools*. Alexandria, VA: Association for Supervision and Curriculum Development.

McKeown, Margaret G., and Isabel L. Beck. 2004. "Direct and Rich Vocabulary Instruction." In *Vocabulary Instruction*, edited by James F. Baumann and Edward J. Kame'enui, 13–27. New York: Guilford Press.

Moll, Luis C., Cathy Amanti, Deborah Neff, and Norma Gonzalez. "Funds of Knowledge for Teaching: Using a Qualitative Approach to Connect Homes and Classrooms." *Theory Into Practice* 31, no. 2: 132–141.

Nagy, William. 2005. "Why Vocabulary Instruction Needs to be Long-Term and Comprehensive." In *Teaching and Learning Vocabulary: Bringing Research to Practice*, edited by Elfrieda H. Hiebert and Michael L. Kamil, 27–44. Mahwah, NJ: Lawrence Erlbaum Associates.

Nagy, William, and Dianna Townsend. 2012. "Words as Tools: Learning Academic Vocabulary as Language Acquisition." *Reading Research Quarterly* 47, no. 1: 91–108.

National Academies of Sciences, Engineering, and Medicine. 2017. *Promoting the Educational Success of Children and Youth Learning English: Promising Futures*. Washington, DC: The National Academies Press.

National Center for Education Statistics. "National Assessment of Educational Progress." Accessed July 11, 2018. https://nces.ed.gov/nationsreportcard/.

Project GLAD®. 1990. Be GLAD LLC. Last updated 2018, https://begladtraining.com/about.

Renzulli, Joseph, and E. Jean Gubbins. 2009. *Systems and Models for Developing Programs for the Gifted and Talented.* Waco, TX: Prufrock Press.

Saunders, William, Claude Goldenberg, and David Marcelletti. 2013. "English Language Development: Guidelines for Instruction." *American Educator* 37, no. 2 (Summer): 13–25.

Schleppegrell, Mary J. 2003. *Grammar for Writing: Academic Language and the ELD Standards.* Davis: University of California, Davis.

Schleppegrell, Mary J. 2004. *The Language of Schooling: A Functional Linguistics Perspective.* Mahwah, NJ: Lawrence Erlbaum Associates.

Swain, Merrill. 1985. "Communicative Competence: Some Roles of Comprehensible Input and Comprehensible Output in Its Development." In *Input in Second Language Acquisition*, edited by Susan M. Gass and Carolyn G. Madden, 235–253. Rowley, MA: Newbury House.

Troia, Gary. 2014. *Evidence-Based Practices for Writing Instruction* (Document No. IC-5). Retrieved from University of Florida, Collaboration for Effective Educator, Development, Accountability, and Reform Center: http://ceedar.education.ufl.edu/tools/innovation-configurations/.

Valenzuela, Angela. 1999. *Subtractive Schooling: U.S.-Mexican Youth and the Politics of Caring.* Albany: State University of New York Press.

Vygotsky, Lev S. 1978. *Mind in Society: The Development of Higher Psychological Processes.* Cambridge, MA: Harvard University Press.

Zwiers, Jeff. 2008. *Building Academic Language: Essential Practices for Content Classrooms.* Newark, DE: International Reading Association.